For Amelia

James O. Speed

The Apostles' Creed

Fresh Water from an Ancient Spring

The Apostles' Creed

Fresh Water from an Ancient Spring

by

James O. Speed

CHEROKEE PUBLISHING COMPANY

Atlanta, Georgia

1988

Library of Congress Cataloging-in-Publication Data

Speed, James O., 1930–
  The Apostles' Creed.

  Includes index.
    1. Apostles' Creed—Sermons. 2. Presbyterian Church—Sermons.
  3. Sermons, American. I. Title.
  BT993.2.S74   1987   238'.11   87-15772
  ISBN 0-87797-144-7 (alk. paper)

This book is printed on acid-free paper which conforms to the American National Standard Z39.48-1984 *Permanence of Paper for Printed Library Materials*. Paper that conforms to this standard's requirements for pH, alkaline reserve and freedom from groundwood is anticipated to last several hundred years without significant deterioration under normal library use and storage conditions. ⊗

Manufactured in the United States of America
First Edition
ISBN: 0-87797-1144-7
91 90 89 88   10 9 8 7 6 5 4 3 2 1
Edited by Alexa Selph
Design by Paulette Lambert

 Cherokee Publishing Company is an operating division of The Larlin Corporation, P.O. Box 1523, Marietta, GA 30061

CONTENTS

FOREWORD

Jim Speed is the best preacher I have ever heard. I recognized it when I transferred my membership to his church in 1982—and I believe it today.

In fact, he's *so* good that it seemed a shame that his sermons could be enjoyed only by members of his church congregation. I even found myself wishing that I could call back the years when I had not been a member at First Presbyterian so that I might hear those sermons that I had missed out on. When I shared this thought at a meeting of the church Worship Committee, I found that others felt as I did, and forthwith I was appointed chairman of a subcommittee to consider the possibility of publishing a collection of Dr. Speed's best sermons.

Jim preaches without a prepared text—or even notes— and this could have been an insurmountable obstacle to the committee's efforts. We were delighted to discover, however, that beginning in 1972, Jim's sermons were taped as they were delivered and later transcribed for the benefit of shut-ins and church members who happened to be absent on a given Sunday. Thus fell to me the pleasant duty of reading through these transcripts, allowing me in a sense to call back those years that I had missed.

The only difficulty arose in choosing from among literally hundreds of excellent sermons. I read and reread the transcripts of these sermons, and found myself drawn again and again to a series of sermons on the Apostles' Creed. At first, I set these aside in the "maybe" stack, and each night added more to be considered later by the full committee.

The more I read, the more convinced I became that the Apostles' Creed series cried out to be shared with a wider audience. Even though the written word lacks the human element so crucial to the communication of a sermon, one cannot read these sermons without getting a sense of the man who delivered them—a sense of his speech patterns and vocal delivery, as well as a sense of himself as a spiritual leader. As I reread each of the sermons in the series, I discovered that they were having a subtle impact upon my life. The act of repeating the Apostles' Creed each Sunday was transformed from a repetitive routine into a sincere commitment of faith, and I found the Creed to be a natural starting point for Christian witness to my friends and associates—something I had been unable or unwilling to do before.

Whether you are struggling with your own personal beliefs as they relate to Christianity, or whether you are seeking confirmation of an already firm faith, I think you will find here, as I did, new life and new meaning in those words that we say every Sunday, those words that we know so well as the Apostles' Creed.

Robert E. Brown

PREFACE

These sermons on an old theme were delivered in one of the oldest functioning church buildings in Georgia. In 1854 the sturdy masonry walls, which are four feet thick, were erected. The structure was roofed and decorated with simple millwork. A prosperous and confident Presbyterian congregation built for growth and quality. The recently uncovered heart pine floors and Pompeiian red plastered walls still make a fine sound chamber for singing songs of praise and for preaching the gospel without amplification. But in the early years, those now polished floors absorbed the scuffing of the muddy boots of Marietta's pioneers, and for a time, the blood of wounded soldiers. Both Confederate and Union armies used the sanctuary as a hospital after the fateful battles fought near Marietta and Atlanta during the summer of 1864.

The postwar years and the periods of depression and change in the South were not easy, but a faithful people continued—held steady by the Christian conviction of those who came before. At least since the 1930s, and probably since long before that, bedrock faith has been articulated and reaffirmed in the Apostles' Creed, a way of expressing the essentials of the Christian faith for over fifteen hundred years. Preaching from the church's ancient creed towards the problems of modern people seems especially fitting in an old building where people seek to hear and increase faith for today.

The Creed is peculiarly the church's document, for the Apostles' Creed did not come from the pen of one writer or even from a particular group. The Twelve Apostles of Jesus never even saw it. Rather, the articles of the creed were collected slowly as churches tried to tell new believers exactly what the apostles taught. The Twelve had been with Jesus in Galilee and Jerusalem. They heard what he said. They saw what he did. They witnessed the resurrection. They preached what they had seen and heard. People believed and were baptized. Churches were formed in the East and then in Athens and Rome, and as far away as Gaul and Britain on the good news the apostles had taught.

In time, the first generation of Christians—including the apostles—died and could no longer be heard or consulted. Church leaders, who sought to guarantee that new converts—including the children—would know and believe the truth about Jesus, began to make lists of the articles of faith that the apostles had taught. The earliest statement may simply have affirmed "Jesus is Lord." (I Corinthians 12:3) But they soon realized that something needed to be said about crucifixion, resurrection, the role of Mary, life after death, and other concerns. The lists grew, and as they grew, they tended to differ from one another. For instance, "He descended into hell" was not on many early lists and still is the most controversial of the articles. The process of testing and refining continued for hundreds of years, until about 500 A.D. By that time, most new believers were repeating the same phrases we know today.

Over the years preachers have stood in pulpits in Roman basilicas, in Greek monasteries, in Gothic cathedrals, and in Puritan meetinghouses to interpret and apply the basic core of the church's ancient faith to meet the temptations, griefs, and challenges of the particular times. These sermons represent one preacher's efforts to stand in an old church and to follow in that old, noble, and necessary tradition.

It should be noted that most good sermons—at least from this preacher's perspective—are not topical, but expository. That is to say, sermons should be honest efforts to explain and apply what some passage of Scripture reveals, not simply the thoughts of other writers and the personal ideas of the preacher. My intention, I hope at least partially fulfilled, was to select a passage of Scripture that expounded more fully the idea or event abbreviated in the Creed. Where possible, I then built the sermon upon the biblical text rather than upon my own collected notions about the phrase in the Creed.

It is also worth noting that the sermons were preached

at a particular time—the winter and spring of 1977. The events and issues of that time provided the raw material for many illustrations and allusions.

Since it seemed best to let the sermons keep their original flavor and life, and since the then-contemporary applications still seem to be intelligible, I let them stand as written.

Books are not brought off the press singlehandedly, especially not books of sermons. Ten years ago David Mahan was faithfully recording my sermons on tape and the then-church secretary, Eleanor McLean, was carefully transcribing them for local distribution—neither of them dreaming they would see their work in print. Pat Thomas, my present secretary, carefully prepared and corrected the manuscript. My wife, Flora, heard every single sermon the night before it was preached and improved more than a few with her suggestions. My friend Bob Brown was generous enough of spirit to believe that a book of my sermons should be printed, and badgered me into getting them ready. I am grateful to them all. Moreover, the congregation of the First Presbyterian Church has given me repeated evidence that all preaching is a two-way proposition. Their support, active encouragement, and expectant listening for the Word of God from the pulpit have provided the only kind of context in which genuine preaching can occur.

Most of all, I thank God for whatever of his gifts are found to be displayed here.

James O. Speed

We believe in one God,
    the Father, the Almighty,
    maker of heaven and earth,
    of all that is seen and unseen.
We believe in one Lord, Jesus Christ,
    the only Son of God,
    eternally begotten of the Father,
    God from God, Light from Light,
    true God from true God,
    begotten, not made, one in Being with the Father.
    Through him all things were made.
    For us men and for our salvation
        he came down from heaven:
(Bow) by the power of the Holy Spirit
        he was born of the Virgin Mary, and became man.

(Genuflect on Christmas and the Annunciation of the Lord.)

For our sake he was crucified under Pontius Pilate;
    he suffered, died, and was buried.
    On the third day he rose again
        in fulfillment of the Scriptures;
    he ascended into heaven
        and is seated at the right hand of the Father.
He will come again in glory to judge the living and the dead,
    and his kingdom will have no end.

We believe in the Holy Spirit, the Lord, the giver of life,
    who proceeds from the Father and the Son.
    With the Father and the Son he is worshiped and glorified.
    He has spoken through the Prophets.
    We believe in one holy catholic and apostolic Church.
    We acknowledge one baptism for the forgiveness of sins.
    We look for the resurrection of the dead,
        and the life of the world to come. Amen.

The Apostles' Creed

I believe in God the Father Almighty, Maker of heaven and earth;

And in Jesus Christ His only Son our Lord; who was conceived by the Holy Ghost, born of the Virgin Mary, suffered under Pontius Pilate, was crucified, dead, and buried; He descended into hell; the third day He rose again from the dead; He ascended into heaven, and sitteth on the right hand of God the Father Almighty; from thence He shall come to judge the quick and the dead.

I believe in the Holy Ghost; the holy Catholic Church; the communion of saints; the forgiveness of sins; the resurrection of the body; and the life everlasting. Amen.

I Believe . . .

Genesis 15:1-6

John 3:1-21

The wind blows where it wills, and you hear the sound of it, but you do not know whence it comes or whither it goes; so it is with every one who is born of the Spirit.

—John 3:8

I Believe . . .

Every Sunday morning we stand in this place and repeat these words:

> I believe in God the Father Almighty, Maker of heaven
>   and earth;
> And in Jesus Christ His only Son our Lord . . .

And then, in measured cadences we proceed in phrase after phrase to repeat the words of the Apostles' Creed.

The word *creed* comes from the Latin verb *credo* (I believe). Thus when you stand and repeat (with some meaning, I hope) a creed, you begin with the straightforward phrase "I believe." The creed that follows is literally what you believe.

Two or three years ago for a season we deleted the Apostles' Creed from the bulletin, partly to keep us from just repeating words without meaning. Not many weeks passed before several individuals asked that it be put back in. They felt it was important to them to reaffirm their faith along with others as a part of worship on Sunday morning. So we re-inserted the Creed. Not many weeks passed before several others came and said, "Why do we have to stand and say all these words? I am not sure I believe every phrase. Isn't it hypocritical to repeat such things without believing them?" Then as a direct consequence of the Creed's being there and provoking questions, we began to discuss this Jesus Christ whom we affirm in the Creed and what he means in our lives. It is important to affirm what we believe in order to think about what we believe.

I remember an experience in a church youth conference several years ago. If you have ever been to a church youth conference, you remember what a communion service on the last night really means to those who participate. Several hundred young people will have worked together, played together, sung together, and eaten together for a week or more. Most particularly, they will have worshiped together and prayed together and struggled together over the meaning of faith until there develops a kind of camaraderie in Jesus Christ, though they may not put it that way, and a special trust in each other and in the adult leadership. They discover that their leaders are not there so much to tell them what to do and believe as to help them think and struggle for themselves. We had come to that time that particular week. As darkness approached, two of us were preparing the communion elements in the chapel. Another leader came up to help. He told us something that had just occurred. One of the boys in his group had come to him privately just before supper that night and said to him, "Now tell me again what this communion business means. What is this Lord's Supper?" This boy was a member of the church—a communing member. He had been to the Lord's Table before. And he was saying, "Tell me again. What does it mean? I need to know because I have made up my mind not to do anything else that I don't believe in."

What you believe is awfully important—perhaps the most important thing that could be said about you or observed in you—because what you believe is eventually what you will be and what you will do.

In these next weeks—indeed, it will go into several months—I want us to look together and think together and pray together and discuss together the core elements in what we believe—not what we believe as Presbyterians particularly, but what we believe as Christians. I want us to look at this Apostles' Creed, phrase by phrase from the perspective of its biblical background, because we do need periodically, week by week, to stand and affirm to ourselves and to others: "This is what I believe." We also need from time to time to examine what we say we believe, lest we speak falsely to God and to others. We also need to look at what we believe in order that we proceed to do what we believe, or, if there are practices we do not believe in, to cease from doing them.

A very long time ago when the Son of God walked upon the earth and was jostled by the crowds, pulled by those who wanted to be healed, and pressed by those who wanted to hear his teachings, he seldom could talk to an individual alone. One particular man made the effort to seek Jesus out alone at night. This was an educated man, an intelligent man, a religious man. He was an important man in his community. He was a leader. His name was Nicodemus. I have a strong suspicion that Nicodemus was the kind of man who knew exactly what he believed— until on a dusty street in Jerusalem he came face to face with a carpenter from Nazareth called Jesus. When Nicodemus began to hear clearly what Jesus was saying and to get some notion of what he was doing and who he was, Nicodemus realized he was going to have to change what he believed. Wise man that he was, he went to that one who was the reason for the change. He started with a tentative affirmation, "We know you are the one who comes from God."

If you have never fully settled what you believe in light of the fact of Jesus Christ, or if you have never fully settled what you do or how you live in light of what you believe about Jesus Christ, then Jesus' responses to what Nicodemus needed to believe may be of help to you.

In the first place, Jesus told Nicodemus that to believe is to be born again. To believe is to start over, to lay new foundations. To believe, Nicodemus, is to reconstruct your life. To believe is to take the building blocks of your life—all its parts that fit together—take them all apart and lay them aside and build them up again on a new foundation, according to a new structural design. To believe, Nicodemus, is to disconnect all the wires of your life and to rewire your life according to a different electrician's plan. To believe, Nicodemus, is to terminate every one of your friendships and to renew all of your relationships with every person on a different basis. That which is of the flesh is flesh, Nicodemus. That which is of the Spirit is spirit. When you were born the first time, when you were born physically, you were nourished and kept alive by milk and by love. But it was human milk and it was human love. All this is wonderful and beautiful and necessary. It is the foundation for human physical and emotional life. You can't live without milk when you are a baby, and you can't survive without love. The doctors call it "failure to thrive," I think, when a baby dies without care. But when you believe, Nicodemus, you must be fed and nourished on what Paul calls "the milk of the Word," the Word that comes from God. You must be nourished on the love not of a mother, but of God himself revealed in Jesus Christ, dying on the cross. When you believe, Nicodemus, you set a new basis for life, upon the Word, the truth, and upon divine love in Jesus Christ.

Many of you have read the novel by Lloyd C. Douglas, *The Robe.* Probably most of you have seen the movie. You will remember that Marcellus was a bright, aggressive young Roman noble. It fell his lot to command the forces that took Jesus to the cross and crucified him. By the casting of lots, Marcellus—according to the novel—was the man who received the seamless robe that Jesus wore. The robe became somehow almost a supernatural symbol of the horror of crucifying this innocent man. Marcellus nearly went mad in the possession of it until he came to accept the realization that this was his Lord and his Master, who somehow had died for him. There is a moment where Marcellus, half in prayer and half in pledge, half aloud and half silently, says to himself something like this:

> He is my Lord. I pledge to him my sword, my treasure, and my sacred honor.

That's what being born again means. That's what believing means. It means that I place into his hands my whole capacity to defend myself and to take aggressive action against any other person. I put that—my sword—in his hands to command. I turn over to him my checkbook, and all of my financial resources, my capacity to feed and house myself and my family. I trust to him my treasure. And I begin to esteem his reputation among others more highly than my own. I pledge to him my sacred honor. That's what it means to believe. It means to stake one's life upon what one says. When one says, "I believe," it means to be born again, to be reconstituted, to start again on a different foundation. I pledge to him my sword, my treasure, and my sacred honor.

Then again, to believe is to take risks, for to believe is not to *know*. Belief is not like saying there is wood in this pulpit, or there is carpet on the floor, or the sun is shining outside, as it appears to be. To believe is to take a step in the dark. Nicodemus kept trying to keep the conversation on a very practical level that he could control with his intelligence: "How can a man be born anew when he is old? Can he enter again into his mother's womb?" A very practical, if ironic, question. But Jesus stayed on the level of the symbolic and of the supernatural. "Those who are born again must be born of water and the Spirit. That which is of the flesh is flesh, that which is of the Spirit is spirit." Then he began to talk to Nicodemus about the wind. You can feel it on your face, Nicodemus. You can see its effects in the clouds or in the sails of a boat, or rustling through the trees. But you do not know where it comes from or where it goes. We know now a great deal more about weather. We have meteorologists today. But when the wind blows the snow south of Atlanta and not on us, there is nothing we can do about it. We still can't control the wind. You see, the person whose trust is in the Lord Jesus Christ, the person who believes, can be blown anywhere the Lord God chooses to blow him, because the Spirit of God is like the wind. We can neither control its source nor its destination. When you say, "I believe," you put your hand in the hand of the Lord. You step out not knowing if the stepping stone is there under the water, but trusting that it will be there when you put your foot down. To believe is to take risks.

And then to believe, as Jesus pointed out, is to respond to God beyond and above anything or anybody else. Jesus himself always made it very clear that he was directing the other person's response not to himself alone, but to God. He told them:

> We have told you those things we have seen and know. That is what we speak about. No one knows about God—no one has ascended up there to see heaven—except he who has descended—the Son of Man.

Then he went on to recall a situation that Nicodemus would know very well. At the time of Moses in the wilderness, there was a plague of serpents—poisonous snakes. God commanded Moses to fashion a bronze serpent and twist it around a pole to give people something to look at, to remind them. He was to walk out into the camp with the bronze serpent lifted up, and those who saw it and believed that God would cure them would recover from the bites of the snakes. Those who believed in God were made well. The plague passed away. Jesus said, "And as Moses lifted up the serpent in the wilderness, so must the Son of Man be lifted up, that whoever believes in him may have eternal life." He was not pointing to himself, but to God, who is beyond him, to whom even Jesus prayed. Our response of faith must always be to God, whom Jesus reveals and to whom he points.

Dr. Felix Gear of Columbia Seminary used to like to point out the difference between the Nicene Creed and the Apostles' Creed in their affirmations about the Church. The Apostles' Creed states, "I believe in the holy catholic Church." The Nicene Creed is more careful. The Nicene Creed states, "I believe one Holy Catholic and Apostolic Church." Not "I believe in . . . ," but "I believe . . . ." In other words, the Nicene Creed says, "We believe the message, the gospel, the good news of Jesus Christ proclaimed by the Church, but we take this human-divine institution, the Church—as highly as we affirm it—with something of a grain of salt. Our faith is in God, not in the Church."

As a young man—in my late teens—I wanted very badly to accomplish goodness. I wanted to be both right and righteous. I wanted God to help me, but I wanted to do it myself. I prayed very hard, "God, help me to be good. Help me to be pure. Help me to do everything you want me to do." Then I couldn't even remember to try. It was only when I began to say, "Lord God, I can't do it. I can't on my own be the man you want me to be. Help me. Forgive me. I am making a mess of it," that somehow— sort of behind the scenes without my knowing it—God began to turn me around. That's why there are certain hymns of great affirmation that have great meaning for me, hymns such as Calvin's hymn:

I greet Thee, who my sure Redeemer art,
My only Trust and Saviour of my heart. . . .

and the one which we will sing in a little while:

Be Thou my Vision, O Lord of my heart;
Nought be all else to me, save that Thou art. . . .

Your belief is always a response—not to an organization, not to any human person, certainly not to oneself, not even to Jesus Christ by himself—but through Jesus Christ to God.

Finally, to believe is to begin to live forever.

John said, "For God so loved the world that he gave his only Son, that whoever believes in him shall not perish, but have everlasting life. . . ." And to make it very clear, he pointed out the contrast—that there are only two ways to live: to believe or not to believe. Those who believe are alive and shall live forever. Those who do not yet believe are not in limbo, they are already condemned. They are damned because they do not believe in the only Son of the living God. That is not to say that they are necessarily damned forever, or that they can't turn and respond and believe, but it is to say there is no middle ground. You either believe or you do not believe. If you believe you are alive, and you live life in a different way, you see things that are not otherwise seen. You still live in a world in which there is pain and suffering, in which some people seem to live by getting other people, in which there are calamities and disasters, in which you have to get up and go to work and go to school on Monday, in which people toil and sweat, and in which they die. Even though all of that goes on, you live knowing that you will live forever, regardless of what anybody does to you, regardless of what happens. You begin to live, noticing that each of these other persons will live forever, either in the agony of alienation from God or in the joy and peace of his presence.

I was reminded again, watching the inauguration parade Thursday, that the newsmen have little "bugs" in their ears. They wear those little speakers like hearing aids. Somebody—the anchor man or the engineer or another reporter—can tell them what is happening that they might not be able to see for themselves. Consequently, the reporter along the parade route could know what was coming, when all of the people around him would have to wait for it to happen. When President and Mrs. Carter got out of the limousine and began to walk, almost instantaneously all the reporters knew about it. Their little "bugs" were working. But the people around had to wait until they saw it, or until the rumor got through the crowd.

You see, believing is having the special speaker in your ears. You know what others do not know. You know some things that others may not discover for years. You know some things they may die before they ever learn—unless you tell them. You know that in the midst of the toil and agony and defeat Christ walks, and there is triumph and life. To believe is to begin to live forever.

At the camp, the young people and adult leaders began slowly to gather for the Lord's Supper, as was the custom, in silence. I, along with the others, could not help but be alert as to whether the young man who had asked the question of belief would come. After a little while, he did. Very deliberately, but quietly, he sat down beside the leader who had responded to his question. As we served the bread and wine, I noticed out of the corner of my eye that he took the bread and ate it. He took the wine and drank it. He had decided what he believed. Once he had made the decision as to what he believed, he came along with the others and committed his life again to Jesus Christ around the Lord's Table.

What do you believe? What are you doing about it?

I *Believe in God*

Psalm 8

I Corinthians 13

*A*nd if I have prophetic powers, and understand all mysteries and all knowledge, and if I have all faith, so as to remove mountains, but have not love, I am nothing.

—I Corinthians 13:2

I Believe in God

"Our wisdom consists almost entirely of two parts: Knowledge of God and of ourselves." With these words John Calvin began the *Institutes of the Christian Religion*. This comprehensive volume on the Christian faith has been the foundation of Presbyterian belief and of enormous influence on Christian thought in general.

Near the opening of our Declaration of Independence, Thomas Jefferson wrote, ". . . that all men are created equal, that they are endowed by their Creator with certain unalienable Rights, that among these are Life, Liberty, and the pursuit of Happiness."

The Christian missionary Paul wrote, "If I speak with

tongues of men and of angels, but have not love, I am a noisy gong or a clanging cymbal."

Each in his own way was contradicting the common notion of American pluralism that "it doesn't matter what you believe, as long as you believe something." Polls reveal that high percentages of our population believe in God. It is also evident that they do not all believe the same things about God, or always in the same god.

Some believe in the God who is the only explanation for a beautiful sunset or a majestic mountain range and who is experienced with a kind of aesthetic awe on beholding such beauty. But this God is not very kind. Those same forces that lift up mountain ranges also produce devastating earthquakes in populated places. This God is no ever-present help in trouble. He *is* trouble.

There are others with scientific and mathematical minds. Their logic drives them to assume a first cause behind the whole system of cause and effect which operates in the physical world. God becomes a name for the whole system. To pray to him would be like praying to a set of geometry theorems.

To still others God seems to be a kind of super granddaddy in the skies. He is the "Man Upstairs," the "Someone Up There Who Likes Me." He looks after you in a loose-reined kind of way. He doesn't look too closely. When something bad happens, he is nowhere to be found.

There are others, and other combinations, but let's look at only one more example. This attitude is expressed by those who say, "Well, we are all trying to get to the same place." That means it does not matter whether you are a Christian or a Jew or a Hindu or a Muslim. We all worship the same God. This is true, but it is very hard to obey a god who commands at the same time: "Love your enemies," and "Kill the infidels."

When things seem to be going well, when you are young and full of vigor, it is easy to be tolerant about what God is like—with others and with yourself. (This is not to say that things always go well for those who are young and full of vigor. Sometimes they go very badly for them.) But when things are going well, some are inclined to think, "Well, it's all right what kind of god anybody believes in. In fact, it's all right for me to have a different god for every day of the week, according to how I feel. It really doesn't matter very much." But when the hard dilemmas and irreconcilable hurts emerge that are beyond the easy answers, then you are pushed to make decisions. You ask, "What kind of person am I? I don't have any rules, I don't know what to do, nobody is here to tell me, but I have got to do something I can live with. What kind of person am I?" Then you are pushed to say, "Who made me? Who put me here? Who runs this life?" And you can't answer the questions of life without saying, "What god is it we worship? What god stands back there behind all of this? Who is it that rewards and punishes? Who makes it all happen? What is he like?"

In the 1770s when the American colonists were increasingly approaching the place where they could not be reconciled to the mother country, England, and to its king, George III, the same kind of question was imposed upon them. "What do you believe about God?" They may not have put it this way, but look at it from this point of view: if they had believed in a God who cared greatly about some people and made them kings, and cared moderately about some others and made them nobles, and sort of cared about some others and made them common people, and didn't care at all about the slaves, there never would have been a Declaration of Independence. We would probably still be citizens of the British Empire. But these colonists had been taught and preached to for generations about the God of all who cares about everybody. It doesn't take much imagination to see how you go from understanding that God cares about everybody to saying that God created all men equal, or at least of equal importance. Then you are able to declare your independence and build a new kind of nation.

It matters what you believe about God, for what you believe about God determines what you believe about yourself. So when we stand and say the familiar words of the Apostles' Creed, "I believe in God," we are not called upon to stand with all the Buddhists and the Hindus and all the people who worship the "Man Upstairs," and just simply say, "I believe in whatever anybody believes about God." We are talking about something very specific, somebody very specific. We are talking about the God that Karl Barth speaks of, "The God in the Highest." He is not the God who can be known by the mathematicians or the scientists. He is not the God who rewards those who do nice things. He is not the God who can be seen so easily in the glow of the red sunset (though that does say something about him). This "God in the Highest" is virtually unknowable by any kind of human means. We can know him, not as we seek him out and find him, or as we think him up, but as he reveals himself to us, and only that way.

We are most open to this revelation of himself—to his letting himself be known—when we run afoul of those kinds of problems and dilemmas and hurts to which there is no easy and really known human solution. Then we are ready to plead, "God, tell me what you are like, so that I can know what I am like."

I think it is helpful to make a careful study of how one particularly thoughtful Christian dealt with a human problem, and to see from that the difference it makes to know who God is and who you are.

Paul had heard about the division in the church at Corinth in Greece. Some of the people were speaking in tongues and they were practicing this in such a way that they let it be clearly known to the others, "We are the superior Christians. We are those who have the higher gifts. The rest of you have just not attained to where we are." I can imagine that some of the others said some equally nice things back to them. The church was beginning to be divided. There were attitudes of bitterness and accusation, and probably the Christian witness in the city of Corinth was just about down around zero. So Paul wrote a letter.

Paul could have started off by saying, "You are arrogant. You are bigoted. You are close-minded. You are self-righteous. You are just plain ugly to each other." He could have accused them. But he didn't do that, though both sides probably deserved it. He could have told them what they ought to do. All of us have a fine proclivity for telling other Christians what they ought to do, don't we? He could have said, "You ought to be kind. You ought to understand your divisions. You ought to be compassionate. You ought to be loving one another. Now, you people get out there and love each other, and you will be all right." He didn't do that, either.

What Paul did was to display something about himself—not to display himself, but to display the true nature of God through himself. He wrote what was very true, very important, and very loving to these people in Corinth. He said, "Look—you all believe in Christ, so you all have the Spirit of God. All of you possess gifts of the Spirit. All of you are a part of the Body of Jesus Christ—the Church. You are important to him, important to the Church, important to me. You are magnificently, wonderfully important. The Body couldn't do without each of you." After he had expressed his words of love for them, about how important each of them was (with, of course, the hint that if you are important, so is your brother and so is your sister), then he went on to talk about what kind of persons they needed to be.

Even this he did gently. He did not say, "Now if you have prophetic powers and understand all mysteries, and if you have all faith so as to remove mountains, but if you don't have love, you are nothing." He didn't say that. He said, "If *I* have prophetic powers, if *I* understand all mysteries and all knowledge, if *I* have all faith so as to remove mountains, but have not love, then *I* am nothing." He let them draw the conclusion themselves about themselves. If they did not have love, they would be nothing.

The kind of person you need to be in order to make the Church work—and really to make life work—is a loving kind of person. Paul went on with some abstractions to describe that. He did not lay it as a heavy load upon these readers. He described it. Look at it. See if you want to be this way. Love is patient and kind. Love is not jealous or boastful; it is not arrogant or rude. Love does not insist on its own way; it is not irritable or resentful; it does not rejoice at wrong, but rejoices in the right. And then love, in spite of all, endures. Love goes on, in spite of all challenges and conflicts. It cannot be killed.

Now, the kind of person you are is what determines what you do when you don't have any rules to follow and don't have anybody there to tell you. For instance, if your son throws a rock through your neighbor's glass window and the neighbor does not know who threw the rock through his glass window, what do you do? There are not any easy rules on that. But if you are a loving person, then you have a particular kind of attitude, a particular kind of methodology, and you desire a particular kind of result. You care about the neighbor and you care about your son. You want your neighbor's best interest to be served, and you want your son's best interest to be served. It is simply not enough for you to look good in the situation. It is simply not enough for your son to look good in the situation. It is simply not enough to pay money and get the window fixed, though that probably will have to be done. If your attitude is love, paying off is not enough. You cannot manipulate anybody, you cannot trick anybody, you cannot hide anything. It may be necessary to punish your son, but simply punishing him is not enough if he does not learn something and if he is not reconciled to your neighbor in the process. You see, love calls for something different. Love calls for something more. And it all depends upon what kind of person you are. And what kind of person you are depends upon what kind of God you believe in.

Paul goes right on in the next step to say, "Love never ends." And when you talk about something that never ends, you are talking about God, aren't you? Prophecies—they are good for this earth, but they will pass away. Tongues—they will cease, for they are only here on earth. All human knowledge is valuable only here on earth. But when you talk about love, you are talking about the nature, the essence of God himself. When the perfect comes, it will be found to be love. When you put away childish things and think like a mature adult, you will find in your maturity that love is what it's all about. You look in a mirror dimly now, but when you see face to face, what you will see is love. When you understand fully as God understands you, you will understand that love is the force that rules the universe. Love has always been in control. Love will one day triumph. Love is an attitude; love is a method; love is a goal; for God is love. That's what it is all about. Those who seek to be like him will live and reign with him forever.

How do I know? How did Paul know? Paul didn't find out that God is love through nature, because nature is not loving. Nature is pretty unforgiving. He didn't find out that God is love through logic—either mathematical or scientific logic—because love is not logical. Logic is a human invention. Love is of God. He didn't find out that God is love through taking the best of all human religions and putting them together. What we learn from human beliefs and behavior is ambiguous, to say the best. Human beings can be cruel and resentful as well as generous and friendly. They are as likely to be hateful or indifferent as to be loving.

Paul found that God is loving—that God is love—because God sent his Son to die for us on Calvary. God loves like that. That is the curtain of heaven opening up for a moment. In the sacrifice of Jesus Christ we see God as he really is. We penetrate to the very essence of God. All other loves—if they amount to anything, if they matter at all—stem from that sacrifice and are measured by it.

You see, this God we talk about in the Apostles' Creed we could not have invented. It would never have occurred to human beings to think up a God who would come in Jesus Christ and sacrifice himself for us. That's what love is about. That's what we couldn't have thought of. We couldn't have seen it in nature; we could not have thought of it in logic; we could not have dreamed it up in our wildest imaginings of a good God. Even the "Man Upstairs" wouldn't have sent his son to die for us. He wouldn't love like that.

When we stand and say the Apostles' Creed, we say again for ourselves and to the world, "The way to live is this: to know God as well as I possibly can, and to do my best to be like him."

Instead of singing our final hymn let us stand and affirm what we believe with the Apostles' Creed.

The Father Almighty

Isaiah 56:1–8

Ephesians 4:1–16

> There is one body and one Spirit, just as you were called to the one hope that belongs to your call, one Lord, one faith, one baptism, one God and Father of us all, who is above all and through all and in all.
>
> —*Ephesians 4:4–6*

The Father Almighty

When Jesus prayed, he called God "Father." When Jesus taught his disciples to pray, he taught them to say, "Our Father." When Jesus spoke of God, he often spoke of him as "the Father," as for instance, "the Father and I are one." The Apostles' Creed first establishes the object of our belief: God. It then states the first title which reveals something of God's character: "Father," or to be more specific, "Father Almighty." It is, I think, typically Christian—in a way that is not typically anything else—to speak of God as "Father."

But what image do you conjure up in your mind when the word *father* is used? Do you picture an individual with white hair, white beard, and a kind of pink complexion, so benign-looking that he could not possibly condemn you except of the most heinous of sins? Or do you think of a strict disciplinarian, as perhaps some of your fathers were or are, one who is the giver and enforcer of rules more than anything else? There are some, of course, who have no really strong, important feeling attached to the word *father* because they lost their fathers to death or divorce when they were small children. And some, of course, have had alcoholic fathers, or fathers who otherwise were abusive, inadequate, inconsistent, or unstable. I have been told that if you deal with certain street gangs in New York City (or elsewhere, for that matter), you do not begin by speaking of God as father, because the image of father in the slums of most cities is very bad.

Some may be offended by the exclusive use of the term for the male parent and, therefore, have problems with the Creed.

In spite of the confusion, we do have some common and useful perceptions that we think of and that we know about. They may not be the most prominent ones in our minds. What we need to look at are the ones that we all know about and the ones that Jesus and the Creed were referring to to draw us towards our understanding of who God may be. I think it is important for us to do this, particularly as we move towards the World Missions Conference, because I think you will discover that as you study the Fatherhood of God, you will find that if God is Father, then you and I are missionaries. That is a kind of logical sequence that we are not accustomed to. Think about that: If God is Father, then you and I are missionaries.

I invite you, then, to look at the fourth chapter of Paul's

Letter to the Ephesians where Paul calls upon the Ephesians to be one, united for the purposes that he has in mind. He begins with the theological understanding that God is Father. He concludes with bodily growth and the upbuilding of the church. Let us see how he got there. Let us see how we can move from an understanding of the Fatherhood of God towards outreach, evangelism, and mission, and a great deal more in between.

The first observation I would make is that if God is Father, then God is a relating God. He is not God who is our Lord by contract or covenant which we have bought or earned. He is one who chooses to be related to us, and to move towards us because of that. Paul says in the Letter to the Ephesians, "There is . . . one God and Father of us all. . . ."

Father is a relationship term. There is, incidentally, no male or female issue here. God is a parent in a family relationship with us. The ancient Greeks were an example that not all people think of God that way. In Greek mythology, gods were those folks who cavorted around on the top of Mount Olympus. They had their own banquets and parties and sports and fetes and had little to do with human beings except for an occasional word after frivolous interventions. There was no natural relationship. Later, as the Greeks moved beyond mythology to an increasingly sophisticated philosophy, they began to think of God as the great principle by which all entities managed to hang together. There was nothing personal here that one could be related to. Even the Hebrews often saw God too much as one who was up there and far off and unreachable. They wouldn't even pronounce his name. When those consonants that we once translated as *Jehovah,* but now as *Yahweh,* appeared in the Old Testament, the Hebrew would not even say the word. He would say *Adonai,* Lord.

Of course, God has been merciful from everlasting to everlasting, and his love is to all generations. We know that now, and the Old Testament says that, but the Hebrew was never quite sure. He always had the feeling somehow that if he abandoned God, God would abandon him—instead of God loving as a Father. It was only in Jesus Christ that we finally have revealed to us in a very convincing way that though we turn away from God, he never turns away from us. Even though we will not serve him or be with him, he never stops loving us.

As great as the idea of the covenant is in the Old Testament and in Presbyterian theology, the idea of the covenant alone is not enough when we think of God. There is a difference between covenanted love, or contracted love, or love resulting as a deal or a bargain, and the love of a father for his child. The love that is made by contract is love that can be broken when the contract is broken, but a parent never stops loving.

When I was a small child I was cared for from time to time by a black maid named Susie. My father paid Susie to come and work for us. A part of her job was to take care of me during those hours that she was there. I grew very fond of Susie. Susie was fond of us. She was exceptionally faithful. But one day Susie didn't show up. When after several days we went to her neighborhood and asked about her, all we could find out was that some relative down in the country had gotten sick and Susie had had to go. We never heard from her again. It would have been nice if Susie had let us know she was going, but Susie was not related to us. When a stronger call came, she abandoned the contract. Fathers and mothers don't do that. You and I occasionally read in the newspapers or hear about a father who does abandon his family, but the reason we hear about it is because it is unusual and abnormal and unnatural. The natural thing is that you love that child because that child is yours.

You will even join the P.T.A. Why in the world do mothers and fathers go to P.T.A.? They would rather be somewhere else. They don't earn anything by doing it. They don't even get better grades for their children. But they are interested in the education process and are concerned to support it, and so they go—because they are fathers and mothers.

Our God is a relating God. He sees himself as a relative. That is part of what fatherhood means.

Further, if God is Father, then God is an intentional God, or if we want to keep it active, an intending God. Paul says, "I therefore . . . beg you to lead a life worthy of the calling to which you have been called."

God is always reaching out through someone toward someone who is lost or separated or confused or wandering about or who has defied God's authority in some way or other. That is what the Prodigal Son did. You and I have a way of backing off and defying the authority of God. Like the Prodigal Son, we go off and waste our substance and God's substance in riotous living. I confess that not too many of you look very riotous this morning. But if you have said to yourself, "I don't need to pray any more," that's riotous living. If you have said, "I will choose my kind of work to do what I want to do and make the kind of money I want to make," that's riotous living. If you have said, "I will choose my mate regardless of the person God leads me to," that's riotous living. If you have said, "I will spend Friday night as I choose to spend Friday night, without even listening for what God may call for me to do," that's riotous living. That is what the Prodigal Son did. He spent his money and his Friday nights as he chose, without reference to God. In the story of the Prodigal Son, the father waited at home and hoped, ready to forgive. But that's not all of God there is. There is also the word from Jesus about the Good Shepherd who leaves the ninety and nine who are healthy and safe in the fold, and goes out and seeks after the one lost sheep. Our God is an intending God—ever seeking out and ever calling. He came in his Son Jesus Christ, and lived as we live, accepted limitations that we have. He hurt as we hurt, cried as we cry, grieved as we grieve, was hungry as we are hungry, suffered on the cross as we would suffer on such a thing, and died the death that we deserve, and then won the victory that we needed so badly, so desperately. You see, God is an intending God, a purposeful God.

Paul, in another place, spoke of "adoption," of God taking us as his sons and heirs—fellow heirs with our Lord Jesus Christ—to emphasize that it is something God intended to do, and not something that just happened. Our God is an intending God.

Then, in the third place, if God is Father, he is a providing God.

We immediately jump to the conclusion, "Well, of

course God in his providence provides us with food and shelter and education and those things as any good father would." But that's really not to the point, or at least that is only the preliminary point. The main point is caught up in the words that Paul uses in talking about this God who is Father in his relation to us: "But grace was given to each of us according to the measure of Christ's gift. . . . And his gifts were that some should be apostles, some prophets, some evangelists, some pastors and teachers, for the equipment of the saints for the work of the ministry, for building up the body of Christ, until we all attain to the unity of the faith and of the Son of God."

God gave every one of us gifts for the sake of someone else. It is even more emphatic if we read the twelfth chapter of Corinthians or the twelfth chapter of Romans. Every good and great gift, even the physical and material ones—but most particularly the spiritual gifts—are for you to have for the sake of someone else.

The church that was put together by the calling of God is not a hierarchy of bishops and apostles and prophets and pastors and teachers and then all those common people at the bottom. The church, rather, is a process in which each individual—pastors, teachers, apostles, whoever—are given gifts for the sake of all the others, so that the church may be equipped for ministry to each other, and finally, to the world out there.

We can learn something from this about human fatherhood and motherhood and what kinds of gifts are really valuable to give our children. You can give your children everything that money can buy, you know, and still fail them. You can give them all the toys, all the clothes, all the automobiles, all the things that they think they want—and still fail them.

In these last weeks since my father passed away, I guess it has been natural that I should think most particularly about my father's life and particularly about that part that touched mine. Because it is important to me, I have asked myself the question, "What did my father give me?" Of course, he gave me the normal things that sustained me and the education that enabled me to do a number of things. I remember the week before he died, he was lying in a hospital bed and apologizing for being, as he said, "a nuisance and a burden to others." I tried in my fumbling way to say to him, "Think about all those years when you worked to provide for Mother and me, and we depended entirely upon you. And think about all those times I had just as soon forget when I was the one who was the nuisance, and you put up with it. It all kind of evens out, doesn't it?" I think maybe that helped. But I know, and I hope he knew, that these were not the greatest gifts he gave me. If I ask, "What did my father give to me?" I would have to answer this way: "He honored God. He loved my mother. He served the church. He responded to the needs of his community in simple, straightforward contributions like First Aid, Lifesaving, and Civil Defense. He cared about people, and particularly about children. And I guess most meaningful to me, he was a man without guile. What he gave to me was something of those parts of him which were useful to other people and to the Kingdom of God. And if I am not as useful as I ought to be or could be, it is not because he did not give me the appropriate gifts."

Our God, if he is Father, is a providing God who enables us to serve and help and reach out. He gives us gifts that are not for us so much as they are for all those with whom we come in contact.

And finally, if God is Father, he is a building God. Or to put it another way, a God who is filling and fulfilling.

The end result of all this activity that puts the church together, that joins it in parts that are knit together—"every joint working properly," as Paul puts it—is bodily growth and the upbuilding of the church. If God is Father, God is a relating God, whose desire it is to be related to every man and woman in the whole of the world and in the whole of the universe—he is the one Father. He is the Father Almighty who is above all and through all and in all. There is no other God, and every person alive is a part of his concern, and one to whom he wants to be Father. It is his manner to be intending, to be purposeful, to be effective in his fatherhood, to reach out through us and others to call all men and women to himself. It is his strategy to be providing, to give to you and to me the kinds of gifts that make us all into that one family of God: nurturing gifts, comforting gifts, supporting gifts, proclaiming gifts, drawing gifts. It is his final purpose to build and fulfill. If God is Father, then you and I are missionaries, because that is what it is all about. That's what is really going on. That's the inevitable result of the nature of God that we are invited to be a part of, that we are called upon to be a part of, that Paul begs us to be a part of. That's really what is happening.

Back in the fall I went to Northcutt Stadium one afternoon to a junior high football game. While the game was being played on the field I noticed that this little group of girls got up and walked over there, and that little group got up down there and walked back up here. This boy got up down here and went over and sat by that person. These three boys went and surrounded that person. One girl who was limping so badly that I just know she must have had a sprained ankle came down the stairs sixteen times in one half! If you think the action at the football game was going on out there on the field, you just really didn't know what was happening.

Do you know what is happening in the family of God? If life just isn't going well for you, if you are trying but you just can't seem to make it, or maybe even worse, if you are getting everything you ever wanted and are finding it empty, maybe this is a good time to stop and consider: What does it mean to me that God is my Father? What is really going on in his household?

Maker of Heaven and Earth

Genesis 1

Romans 8:18–25

And God made the two great lights, the greater light to rule the day, and the lesser light to rule the night; he made the stars also. And God set them in the firmament of the heavens to give light upon the earth, to rule over the day and over the night, and to separate the light from the darkness. And God saw that it was good.

—Genesis 1:16–18

Maker of Heaven and Earth

The subject of the sermon is "God, Maker of Heaven and Earth." For many, the first real discovery of the wonder of God's creation comes in Scout camp or in some kind of Scouting program. For me this is particularly meaningful, because it was at Scout camp that I first stopped and noticed a wildflower. It was at Scout camp that I first discovered that every leaf on every tree is different from every other leaf—even on that same tree—and those on that tree are different from the leaves on some other variety of tree. It was at Scout camp that I first watched the colors of the sunset on the wall of a cliff across the lake. It was at Scout camp that I first began to identify the various birds by their colors and markings. It probably was at Scout camp that I first went to church out-of-doors. I could preach this sermon if I had not been a Scout, but I would not have preached it in the same way.

Toward the end of this past week when this sermon was in progress, I received an exciting telephone message. I learned that one of our college students had been accepted in A Christian Ministry in the National Parks for this summer and will be a part of the ministry team in Yellowstone National Park. Jeannie Ramsey will be a part of a small team in a particular area, and a part of a larger team of over three hundred college and seminary students from across the country in all of the major national parks. That's exciting to me, because twenty years ago and a little more I was in that program myself for about fifteen months: two summers in Crater Lake and the winter in between in Death Valley. It was almost as exciting as if I were going to get to go again. I look forward to the witness that Jeannie will have and to hearing about it.

The key focus of their ministry will be conducting services of worship in the parks for visitors and staff. These services will be in hotel lobbies, in amphitheaters or recreation buildings, around campfire circles, or in any place where permission can be gained and people can be gathered out of the hotels or campgrounds or from those passing through.

Almost every Sunday in Crater Lake and in Death Valley someone coming out of church would remark to me or to one of the other members of the team: "I haven't been to church in maybe ten years. But after seeing that marvelous view out there, I just had to go."

Now what does that mean? Does it mean that the individual has been overwhelmed by the majestic beauty that could only have been created by God, and feels compelled to go and say, "Thank you, God," in the worship service? Maybe that's part of it. I know that I have been outside and have rejoiced in the opportunity to worship in the open air or under the stars and to be able to say thanks on my own to God for the wonder, beauty, and majesty of what I beheld. That's a part of it, certainly, and we need to do that.

I wonder also if it meant that for some, the experience of being awestruck reminded them of the God they had forgotten and neglected for perhaps many years. It then seemed natural and appropriate to go and worship him. I suspect that's a part of it, too.

But there is also a third element. I used to sense it as I stood in a makeshift pulpit and looked at the faces of people, many of whom did not go to church regularly. I sensed a certain kind of openness, a certain readiness to hear what was said from the pulpit, to hear what the Scripture taught as it was read and explained.

Perhaps that's the greatest motivation in those who are overwhelmed with the beauty of what God has created. They find not that they have suddenly discovered all that there is to know about God, but rather they have discovered that God's nature is deeper and greater and more wonderful and more indescribable than they had ever suspected. Rather than feeling satisfied with what they see of the Creator in creation, they are stimulated to go and discover more about this Creator who is even less known as they begin to ponder his being. This is confirmed to me in the fact that in this Christian Ministry in the National Parks some of the strongest, most loyal supporters and faithful participants are the professional National Parks Service people—the naturalists, the rangers, the maintenance people, even park superintendents and their wives and children. Many of these people who live with the wonders of God's creation day after day, week after week, all year, still find that they do not get the answers to what they need to know for their lives about God—even in some of the greatest wonders of the world.

Last summer, my family and I stood on the rim of the Grand Canyon just before sunset and looked down and tried to find the Colorado River, literally a mile below us. Where we stood was, I think, near the beginning of the "Bright Angel" trail, one of the trails that goes down into the canyon. As we stood looking, we saw a young man come out of a little short tunnel about a hundred feet below us near the beginning of the trail. He stepped off the trail and picked his way out onto a point where, I guess, he had a spectacular view of the canyon. He sat down—to think? to meditate? to pray? Was he an employee of the park or of one of the hotels? Did he come there every day? (He looked like he knew what he was doing.) I couldn't help but wonder what he was meditating about. Go to a Scout camp sometime, and if you watch closely, now and again at particular times of the day, you will find one boy or two boys who go by themselves and sit or stand and look and think long thoughts. You know, if you have never done that, you have missed something very important in life. I wondered what this fellow thought about as he looked over the Grand Canyon. Could his thoughts have gone something like this? There is the river down there. There are these thousands of intricately formed valleys and ravines and gaps, all made by water and the action of water and the sand in the water cutting the stone over millions of years. How many thunderstorms were there? How many drops of water? How many times did the same molecules of water go down, cutting the sides of the cliff, into the river and on into the ocean, there to be evaporated and to form clouds again? How many thousands of times did the process have to take place before the Grand Canyon was formed? And, of course, you take into consideration the thrusting upward of the land in earthquakes and volcanic activity, and the time when the Grand Canyon was dammed by lava flow for only five thousand years or so until the water worked through again. You think about all of that, and there *has* to be a God—there just *has* to be.

"The heavens are telling the glory of God, and the firmament showeth his handiwork." And the Grand Canyon, if you will, demands his existence.

But how did he do it? Well, you take out your geology books, and you study about the layers of sedimentation, the hundreds, the thousands, the millions of layers going all the way down to where the river flows. You study about the volcanic activity, you study about the upheavals in the earth that thrust this layer up and that layer down, and set them out unevenly. You keep going down layer upon layer until you come to the place where the earth is a hot mass of matter. Then you set aside the geology books, and you pick up the astronomy books. You read about how these hot gases were hurled out into space by the "Big Bang" they talk about, that one great explosion where it all began, and the planets and the stars were hurled out whirling, until as they whirled they cooled into balls and finally into solid masses. But where did the matter come from? What was the energy that created the "Big Bang" in the first place? The answer you come up with is God. God whom you understand now even less than when you started.

Perhaps the purest of the scientists are the ones most apt to worship God in wonder and in awe, because they know the questions that aren't answered, and for which there are no tools toward answers. God—and we are left to wonder at his being because of what we have seen created—a God we know even less as we ponder what he has done.

And so also with the question, "Why?" Why did he do it?

Last summer on that same adventure, which we sometimes inadequately called a trip, we found ourselves crossing Wyoming at the place near the Continental Divide where the Oregon Trail crosses. We wondered what those people who drove their wagons and walked alongside must have thought when they picked their way through those rock-strewn, rugged valleys with no vegetation except sagebrush and the like, between ragged, arid, treeless hills and cliffs. There they were—sixty days or more out of St. Louis, and not yet halfway to Oregon, in July—hot dusty, barren, and bleak days. Didn't they ask why? Not only "Why am I here?" and "What in the world did I do to bring my family here?" but "What is there to this life that brings me out here? Why did it all come into being in the first place?" And if they had shouted again and again at those barren hills, "Why? Why? Why?" there would have come back the answer of silence. The creation does not tell you why.

And, boys and girls, if you are awake some night camping under the stars and you look at the wide, star-filled expanse (and you can see them all because the lights of the city are not there), you might look up and ask, "Why?" The answer that will twinkle back will be silence, because the stars and the barren hills of Wyoming cannot tell you why.

You will only discover why in Jesus Christ. In almost every place in the New Testament where Jesus' purpose and meaning for being here is told, the creation is in part explained and pointed to. "For God so loved the world, that he gave his only begotten Son . . . ." Isn't that what he has always done—loved the world, from the very beginning?

"God was in Christ, reconciling the world to himself." And if there is reconciliation, there must have been some preexisting state where the warring parties were together. God's original plan and the original state of things between God and his creation, including you and me, was companionship and fellowship and a relatedness to each other. Only out of those circumstances can there be any talk about reconciliation after the companion partners have separated. But God made us for companionship with him. Christ came to restore it. Jesus said, "When the Son of Man is lifted up, he will . . ." What? ". . . draw all men to himself," and, therefore, to God, whose Son he is. The New Testament talks about those who come to Jesus as being called "friends," "heirs," "fellow heirs," "the sons of God." Paul says that the whole creation has groaned in agony up until now for the revealing of these sons of God, these companions, these fellow heirs.

What is it all about? God wanted us to have fellowship with him, and he made the world and put us in it because he loves. God did not need the world. God did not need us. God doesn't need anything. But God desired to have people to love and to love him. And so he made us in love. The very act of creation is an act of God's grace. In quality the act of creation is identical with the act of the giving of his Son to save. Creation is an act of grace.

The theologian Karl Barth has remarked that the more you look at God's creation, the more you are impressed that the wonder is not that God exists—that is obvious— but the wonder is that the world exists, because God did not have to do it. That's the incredible thing—that God in his grace chose to create.

And what did he create? The Scripture tells us and the Creed affirms: the heavens and the earth. There is a reason for distinguishing between the two; for if we say that God created the heavens, then we are saying God is not locked into heaven. God is not someone who was born and raised there and is a child of heaven as you and I are born and raised upon earth. Heaven belongs to God. He made it. All of the denizens of heaven, all of its beings, whether angels or archangels, the good supernatural beings of God, or the evil supernatural beings—all are those who are in being because God made it so, and all are under his control. They either serve him as angels or they are rejected and defeated by him if they are evil supernatural beings. Whatever supernatural state there may be, it is a state that God controls, because he is above it. He made it. It is his. You and I need not be frightened by anything or by any statement or any threats from anybody about the supernatural, because God is in control of the supernatural and he cares for his own.

Furthermore, heaven exists as God's creation alongside this earth that we can see. Perhaps you and I cannot talk about its furniture or its institutions, but if we believe in God, we know it is there. It stands alongside to give us meaning and to give us a place to move toward. Hartzel Spence, in the title of his book *One Foot in Heaven,* was not far wrong, because whenever one in faith begins to obey God and to be a part of his kingdom, that person begins to live in heaven and to know some of its joys. God created heaven for our destiny and our destination. Does that strike you as wonderful that God made heaven for you and me? God did not come out of heaven determined and made by it, but he created it, that you and I would have a place to go.

And also, he created the earth. He is not locked into the earth. He is not trapped on the earth. He is not caught up in or limited by the cause-and-effect laws of the science of the earth. The earth belongs to God. He made it. And he can go beyond the rules that we formulate from what we think we have observed in nature. God is above them, and over them, and is not bound by them. God is not the God of nature. Nature is the creation of God.

If God created all things, then he is the owner of all things. And if he is the owner, then you and I are either stewards or robbers. We either use this creation that he gave us in relationship to him and to enhance that relationship in companionship with him, or we misuse it to our own self-destruction. It is his. He is the owner.

When I played high school football, they gave me a uniform. They gave me a helmet and shoes and pants with pads in them, and shoulder pads and a jersey with a number on it. I was privileged to use that for the sake of the team, even to use it up for the sake of the team. When the season was over, I turned the uniform in. These things were given to be used with the team. God gave us all things to be used in companionship with him, and only that way.

You know, the real choice that you and I have in this life is not between good and evil, between right and wrong. If, with all your wisdom and goodness, you think you can really choose between right and wrong and good and evil, you are playing God, and that's about the most fundamental mistake that we human beings make: to think that we can—as Adam and Eve thought they could, with the tree of knowledge of good and evil—choose between the two without God's presence. That sets us up in God's place. The basic choice of life is between following and trusting God and chaos, between love and obedient companionship with him and slow death to the terrible isolation of hell. The real choice is between God and being and not being at all.

God created the heavens and the earth—for us. I find that simply astounding!

"When I consider thy heavens, the work of thy fingers, the moon and the stars, which thou hast ordained; what is man, that thou art mindful of him? and the son of man, that thou dost care for him?"

Jesus Christ His Only Son Our Lord

Isaiah 42:1–13

Acts 2:14–36

*L*et all the house of Israel therefore know assuredly that God has made him both Lord and Christ, this Jesus whom you crucified.

—*Acts 2:36*

Jesus Christ His Only Son Our Lord

Last week the Anglican Bishop of Uganda was murdered—apparently by the president of his country. Our ambassador to the United Nations, Andrew Young, stated that this is tribal warfare, and that Idi Amin is trying to eliminate the power of the tribes other than his own in that country. We are made to believe by the newspapers that civil war, that can only be called a racial war, is about to break out in the small nation of Rhodesia. If you saw "Roots" on television, you probably felt as never before the horrors of slavery. You also noted that implicated in the slave trade were not only the white slavers and white plantation owners, but also Arab traders and even black African chieftains. Not many weeks ago, Freddie Prinze, of television's "Chico and the Man," took a gun and shot himself.

There is nothing at all unusual about any of this. There is nothing at all unusual about the series of incidents of indiscriminate and useless violence that we have heard about or read about in the newspapers. There is nothing unusual in the history of the world about murder, about violence, about national conflict, about tribal warfare, about suicide. What is unusual is that an ordinary group of fairly prosperous, reasonably comfortable Presbyterian Americans should choose to buy a truck for medical work and spiritual work among people in an area of Central Africa so remote that it takes a four-wheel-drive vehicle to get to most of them.

There is no question but what the world needs to be changed. There is no question but what there are individual lives that need to be changed. How many hundreds and thousands are there like Freddie Prinze who appear to be successful, prosperous, and in control, when really they are coming apart? Maybe you are one of those who straighten your tie, wash your face, or put on your makeup and a good front, when really you are miserable, afraid, and can barely drag yourself out of bed in the morning. You dread the life you will live on that day. There are people who need to be changed. And there are people being changed.

Incredible, that ordinary American Christians will care enough to send doctors into the bush of Central Africa to people they have never seen and never will see! And that's just a tip of what is happening. Do you want to participate in the changes being made? Do you want to take a greater part in changing the lives of those who are miserable inside? Do you want to be changed yourself? Perhaps you are one of those who is already in the process of being changed. You would like to help the process and not hinder it. I invite your attention to where it all began, at the beginning of the Church of Jesus Christ at Pentecost.

The day began with great excitement. All those who had observed the resurrection of Jesus from the dead were gathered together in one place. Suddenly there appeared, as it were, tongues of fire on every head. Then they all began to speak in other languages so that people outside on the street who came from all over the world heard the mighty acts of God proclaimed in their own tongues. There was such an uproar that everybody in the neighborhood ran in to see what was going on. That's how it began. And the day ended with three thousand new Christians attending to the teachings of the apostles, in the fellowship with other Christians, participating in the breaking of bread, and in the prayers.

And, you know, those who are busy about attending to the apostles' teachings and to the fellowship with other Christians, and the rest of it, just aren't going out murdering anybody, promoting national violence, stirring up tribal warfare, or committing suicide. The changes have begun. New lifestyles in the world have come into being.

Now, what really produced the changes? What made it happen?

Certainly not the excitement, and not even the experience of the disciples in speaking in tongues. To be sure, that must have thrust them out with new conviction and new enthusiasm. But the people who heard it and saw it thought they were drunk. Let me tell you that people in the first century A.D. were no more impressed with drunks and what they had to say than you and I are now. That wasn't what did it. Peter got up to speak. It was not Peter's eloquence that did it. All of us have heard people who entertained us and who impressed us with their speaking power who did nothing for us. We listened with interest and we went away the same.

Do you remember what happened when the national cemetery was dedicated at Gettysburg, Pennsylvania, toward the end of the Civil War? You have heard the story. Edward Everett, reputedly the greatest orator of his time, spoke for three hours. (I do not recall ever having seen a single sentence from Edward Everett's address quoted anywhere.) Then President Lincoln stood up, and in a few well-chosen and intensely sincere sentences about what our country is about, spoke to the people gathered. Grade school children still memorize what he had to say in the Gettysburg Address.

It was not the eloquence of Peter, though he may have been eloquent. It was what he had to say. There in that moment, in the fullness of time when the people were gathered with excitement, when the disciples were ready, Peter stood up and told them about Jesus. That's what the Apostles' Creed is about. There are a few short phrases at the beginning about God the Father Almighty, Maker of heaven and earth, and a few short phrases at the end about the Holy Spirit and about the Church. But that great central core is about Jesus. It is through Jesus that we know God, and it is through Jesus that we experience the Holy Spirit. That's what the Christian faith is about. It is about Jesus.

If you want to see the world changed, if you want to participate in the changing of people, if you want to be changed yourself, then make very sure that you understand who Jesus is.

The Apostles' Creed begins it, ". . . Jesus Christ His only Son our Lord." That is a series of names and titles. Let's look at them one at a time as Peter looked at them in his sermon.

Jesus. That was an ordinary masculine name. It was a name that was given to Hebrew boys. In Hebrew it is Jeshua, sometimes translated Joshua. As it goes through the Greek, it comes out Jesus. It means "savior." I am sure that was intentional and significant. But Jesus was not the only little Hebrew boy in Nazareth or in the rest of Judaea and Galilee named Jeshua. There were many of them. It was like John and James and Bill and Bob in our time. The point in the name is that it is a human name and he was a human boy. Peter said, ". . . this Jesus whom you know. . . ." He was a man. He was from Nazareth. They knew the streets he walked on. They knew the house he lived in. They knew where the carpenter's shop was. They knew what his father's heritage was and what his occupation was. They had heard about the mighty works and the wonders and all the signs in Galilee. Some of them had seen them. But they were the signs of a man sent from God—a man: a man who cried, a man who slept, a man who sweated, a man who could hurt, a man who could laugh, and a man, yes, who could die when they nailed him to the cross. He was a man.

Jesus chose for himself and most often used the title, not Son of God, but Son of Man. He identified himself with other human beings. He seemed from the beginning to

identify himself as their representative, as our representative, as the one who being human could take the punishment of human beings and absorb it in himself. As he put
it himself one time, as John remembered, he had to be the
Son of man so that he could make the sacrifice for man.
Never let anybody try to persuade you that Jesus was only
God and a shadowy human being. He was real flesh and
blood. If he were not, the sacrifice would be to no avail. It
was a sacrifice that hurt. The nails hurt him. He died a real
death. He was truly separated from God in it. Jesus, the
Man from Nazareth.

The Christ, the Son of God. Do you remember that great
event in Peter's life that took place in Caesarea Philippi?
Some months before, Jesus had taken the disciples aside—
away from the crowds—and asked, "Who do men say that
I am?"

They answered, "Moses, or Elijah, or one of the prophets."

"But who do you say that I am?" he asked.

Peter blurted it out almost as if it had been rising up
within him, as though he had not really thought it out,
but when the question was asked, he knew: "You are the
Christ, the Son of the living God."

Christ—the Greek word *Christus.* It means "anointed
one." In Hebrew it was *Messiah.* In the Old Testament
times, the Hebrews anointed the people they recognized
as being called out to lead them—called out by God. They
anointed kings. They anointed prophets. They anointed
priests. Sometimes they anointed their teachers of wisdom, and sometimes the ones they called judges. They
were men of God. They ordained them by anointing

them. Then, after the great days of David and Solomon when the kingdom was divided, first one part and then the other went off into exile. When they almost lost hope, the prophets began to tell them there would be one special Messiah, one unique anointed one, one who would restore the glory to Israel—no, would restore Israel to the place where it would again give God the glory. Peter recognized it that day. "You are the Messiah, the only Son of God."

Remember that the Old Testament was the Scripture, the Word of God in the time of Jesus. Long before the New Testament was the Word of God, there was the Old Testament, the Word of God. Every Jew understood that if it were there in the Bible, the Scripture, in the Old Testament, it was so. Even the Gentiles who were sensitive about God looked at it with awe and respect. With all the discussion about David and his recognition of the one to come, and in citing David as a part of the Old Testament, Peter was saying very clearly, "This is the one who has been predicted by all the prophets. This is Messiah, attested by Scripture." And the *only* Messiah; not one Messiah out of many others; not someone made God because God singled him out and pulled him up; not someone who by good works climbed up towards God and was recognized as having reached the high plateau of humanity; but the one sent from God, the only Son of God. Notice that it is not "made by God." The Nicene Creed says, "Not made," (not created) but "begotten" of God's own flesh. A physical extension of God is the illustration. It is a human way of saying, "This is God of very God," as the Nicene Creed says it. Jesus, the Christ, the Messiah, the only Son of God.

Peter caught it, and nothing happened. Isn't that terrible? Peter understood who he was, and he didn't do anything about it. Not many months later, after Peter recognized that this was the very Son of God, he cringed before a little piddling fire in the courtyard of the high priest while Jesus was on trial, and denied him three times.

I think you and I understand that all too well. Isn't it possible for us to give intellectual, mental assent to something, to say, "It is true, but—I don't have to do anything about it right now"? You and I can believe every word in the Bible and still, like Peter, deny our Lord three times.

What then did make the difference? What did produce the changes? The key word is *Lord*. Peter recognized that he whom they killed had been raised from the dead in power. They were all witnesses, and Peter could preach, "Let all the house of Israel therefore know assuredly that God has made him both Lord and Christ." God made him Lord as well as Christ. Jesus who died has been raised from the dead. Having been raised, he rules. He is sovereign. He is king. Let's put it plainly: He is boss. He is Lord.

When you say "Lord," the response is natural. The people around said, "Men and brethren, what can we do to be saved?" Peter told them. Repent and be baptized. That means, "Change." Repent means, "Turn around!" To be baptized means to make the basic commitment of the changed person. It is the initiation into the Christian faith. Be changed.

And what did they do? Where did they begin? How did they start to change? They attended to the apostles' teachings, the fellowship of other Christians, the breaking of bread together, and the prayers. That is the base from which Christian people go wherever God wants them to go and do whatever he wants them to do. From the base of attending to the apostles' teachings, from the base of the Christian fellowship, from the base of the Lord's table where the bread is broken, and from the base of the prayers, we get not murder and violence and national conflict and tribal warfare, useless killing and suicide. We get the buying of trucks for the medical mission in Zaire. We get honesty and witness in business. We get people presuming to teach Sunday School, because they want other adults and children to know Jesus Christ his only Son our Lord. Those who believe that are changing the world.

A few days ago, Dean Rusk was quoted about something he said about a matter that came to his mind in the midst of the Cuban missile crisis, when for a few days we teetered on the edge of World War III. He remembered from his Presbyterian childhood the Shorter Catechism question "What is the chief end of man?" Man's chief end is not to help himself or to save himself. His chief end is to glorify God. It is obedience. It is the recognition of Jesus Christ as Lord and finding the glory of God and serving him. With such convictions peace is made in the world—in the very real world of Soviet ships and nuclear missiles.

Jesus Christ His only Son our Lord. Those who believe that are changing others. It has been a matter of sorry disillusionment for us all to discover again that you can't do business in many parts of the world, presumably, unless some money or service or favor is passed under the table to a government official. It is a sorry thing to know that in some businesses in our own country it is understood that something needs to be passed under the table or business cannot be consummated. But that is not so for everybody, and there are Christian men and women who insist that they will obey Christ, whatever may be the current demands of business. They understand that obeying Christ as Lord in business means that it is all honest and out in the open. Pretty soon others know they stand that way, and begin to ask why and how.

You know, you do not deserve the right to tell other people that Jesus Christ is Lord until you have made him your Lord in such everyday events as how you do business and how you do schoolwork. But those who recognize him as Lord are asked questions, and they have something to say. Men and women are being changed.

Jesus Christ His only Son our Lord. Those who believe that are being changed themselves. You say to yourself, "I don't know what the Lord wants me to do next year. I don't know what he wants me to do with the totality of my life. I don't know how I am supposed to solve this big business crisis or this family problem." There are a great many things you and I don't know right now, and we don't get visions out of the blue that tell us. But you do know what the Lord expects of you now at this moment. If he is Lord of your life, you know what he wants you to do right now.

Notice the central emphasis in the Creed: "Jesus Christ His only Son our Lord." Is he your Lord? It was a long, long way for Peter from Caesarea Philippi through the outer court of the high priest to the day of Pentecost. It was a long, long way from one who could give intellectual assent to the Messiahship of Jesus, the Son of God, through denial, to claim him as Lord of his life.

Where are you in all this? Are you still at Caesarea Philippi, wondering who in the world Jesus is? Are you with Peter in the courtyard of the high priest calling yourself by the name Christian and yet denying him by what you do and what you say in ordinary life? Or are you at Pentecost, claiming him as your Lord, even if that means going to Africa, even if that means teaching a Sunday School class, even if that means talking to your neighbor about who is his Lord and yours, even if that means honesty in business and in schoolwork?

What does it mean to you to say "Jesus Christ His only Son our Lord"?

Conceived by the Holy Spirit

Isaiah 9:2–7

Matthew 1:1–25

*B*ut as he considered this, behold,
an angel of the Lord appeared to him
in a dream, saying, "Joseph, son of
David, do not fear to take Mary your
wife, for that which is conceived in her
is of the Holy Spirit."

—*Matthew 1:20*

Conceived by the Holy Spirit

A television program of some years ago always ended with these words: "There are eight million stories in the Naked City. This has been one of them." Do you remember? I liked that ending because it raised the possibility that for every one of us there is a real, live, breathing story—a story worth telling on television.

There are some forty-odd stories behind that long list of names that appear in our scripture lesson from Matthew. To you and me, they are mostly unpronounceable and forgettable names; but for every name there was a person— a living, breathing human being. There were several women. For every father listed there was also a mother and, probably, other children. For every one of these families there is a story: the struggle to get enough to eat, to find or build a home, to love, to make life interesting and good, to bear sorrow and disappointment, and to enjoy whatever good might come. Forty-odd generations of stories, of people, of the common progression of humanity and flesh and blood descent; son succeeding father and another son succeeding him for hundreds and thousands of years; the common life of humanity, joys and sorrows, triumphs and disappointments, hopes and aspirations and dreams that are dashed and shattered to the earth; human life that goes along ups and downs and sometimes on a plateau; an endless (it seems) succession of births and deaths and births and deaths; and so-and-so begat so-and-so—and on and on.

And at the end of the list—Jesus—placed into the common stream of humanity. Every individual included in the list was important, because if anyone had been left out, if anyone had died early, if anyone failed to marry, the list would have stopped, and so would the list on which you stand. Jesus Christ is at the end of the list of human descent, making every name important.

But as some names are unfamiliar, some are very familiar: Abraham, Isaac, Jacob. You recognize those. You also recognize Judah—not the eldest of Jacob's sons, but somehow the most preeminent. Then David the king, and Solomon, and Josiah, probably the best king after David. The greatness of the Hebrews, the people of God, was yet not only the height, but also the depth; for there was the wretched Jeroboam with his cold, cruel foolishness, as well as other evil kings. This succession of kings is the line in which the Messiah must come. Must the Messiah inherit the evil along with the good? You find the ups and downs and the plateaus that go nowhere in life. Once you reach the heights with David and Solomon, you drop back down again. Thank God that when we come to the end of the list we come to strange and unique wording—and a surprise!

That is why I read it all. Listen: ". . . and Eleazar begat Matthan; and Matthan begat Jacob; and Jacob begat Joseph, the husband of Mary, of whom was born Jesus, who is called Christ." That is not just an accidental insertion of different wording into a consistent genealogical list. The words are chosen with care. This is the only place where a son is listed not as the son of his father, but as the son of his mother. This is an interruption. This is a break, not only in this particular genealogical list in this particular set of ancestors. This is a break in the flesh-and-blood descent of all humanity, for this is the first man who is born of woman but not born of man. This is the first child listed as born not of the flesh and the blood, but of the Holy Spirit. That is a fork in the road. That is a turning point. That is where the channel turns and goes in another direction. That is God's own interruption in human life. Human life had been going along irregularly on this kind of hopeless plane where no one really gets anywhere and everything is repeated over and over again. That is where God interferes and suddenly the direction goes up towards God, towards victory, meaning, and eternity. That's what the Apostles' Creed means when it says that Jesus was conceived by the Holy Ghost. A whole new line of humanity has come into being. A whole new beginning has been made. John, at Patmos, heard our living, reigning Lord say, "Behold, I make all things new." And he does.

As Christ came into the world conceived by the Holy Spirit, he broke into a number of things. He interrupted the tyranny of cause-and-effect. He broke into the scientific inevitability. His birth was an unconnected event by the science of his time or of any time. They didn't know as much about biological science in those days as we do now. They didn't know as much about human reproduction. According to the science of their time, a son had a father. But Jesus was not born of Joseph. That was different.

A number of years ago, L. Nelson Bell, a physician and a missionary, wrote a short article entitled "A Physician Looks at the Virgin Birth"—which also means a look at conception by the Holy Spirit. I don't remember the details of the article, but I remember that there was nothing new or surprising in it, nothing very technical that you or I would have difficulty understanding. There was nothing really for a physician to elucidate. I think that was Nelson Bell's point. You take science as far as it can go; you take engineering as far as it can go; you take technology as far as it can go; you take everything that is observed and put together by the mind of man as far as it can go; and then beyond that, there is the mystery that is God. When we deal with the fact that Jesus was conceived by the Holy Spirit, we are struck with awe. The only way you can handle that is by faith. No scientist can tell you about it; no doctor can describe it for you; no engineer can put it together; no computer scientist can reconstruct it. This only God can do.

Don't you see, that means your prayers are answered. It means that when you have done everything available to medicine and to human science, when you have followed all of the best principles of psychology, when you have built the best building or the best dam or the best road an engineer can construct, when you have done it all with electronics, you haven't arrived at all the answers. You have not explored all the possibilities. Beyond all that is God.

The Lord Jesus Christ was conceived by the Holy Spirit. He was a break with the dominance of science, for science with all its forms is not our master. The Lord God is the master of science, and science is our servant—a useful servant, but still a servant. Science is not our Lord. Jesus is our Lord.

Furthermore, he was a break with the dominance of human history. They call economics the dreary science. History can be a rather dreary subject, too. If you read it in broad sweeps, you read of the rise and the fall of empires. If you read it from the Marxist point of view, everything is determined by economics, and everybody is simply driven by the struggle necessary for getting a loaf of bread or more welfare. If you read it as a search for power, it is a series of just as many dismal failures as glorious successes. Civilizations rise, civilizations fall; powers rise, powers fall; and history goes nowhere.

But, even the most secular historians have difficulty ignoring the difference between B.C. and A.D. Something new came into the world. Something new began to happen with the coming of Jesus Christ.

We may think of the antics of the knights of the Middle Ages as childishly silly and brutal until we compare them with what went before them. The rules of chivalry were certainly an improvement over the savagery of the barbarians of northern Europe before Christ was born there. Even today most of the good and fine institutions that take care of people and heal people find their origins somewhere in the church of Jesus Christ. The American Red Cross still carries the cross which says (whether it intends to or not) where the caring came from. The safety people have long used a green cross as their symbol. Somewhere behind all of these organizations and institutions of good works is Christ. History has been different ever since it was interrupted by the Holy Spirit bringing Jesus into the world.

Jesus, born of the Holy Spirit, was a break also with that kind of psychological determinism that all of us are so familiar with: the idea that we are emotionally programmed by whatever our parents did or did not do to us when we were little children. We owe a great debt of gratitude, I am sure, to Sigmund Freud. He was one of the dominant thinkers of this century. He did get us to believe and understand that mental illness is illness and should be treated that way. He taught us that we are influenced unconsciously as well as consciously by what happened to us in our early childhood and beyond. But it can be taken too far to the point that people believe they cannot be anything but what their parents made them by these unconscious influences. "My mother and daddy did so and so to me, or they didn't do so and so for me, and this is just the way I am. I can't help myself." I have heard it again and again until I am sick of it: "When I was a little boy, they made me go to church, and I just can't go any more." Tommy Smothers made it as a comedian by complaining to his brother Dick, "Mother loved you more than me. She gave me a chicken as a pet instead of a dog." Nonsense!

Jesus Christ was not the son of a human father, and he forever broke the chain of psychological determinism (if it was ever really there). The Holy Spirit enters into the human line of descent. Anyone who will—responding to the love of God in Jesus Christ's living and dying and rising again for us—can be different. You are the way you are because you are either too cowardly to change or you willfully will not change. The Holy Spirit can change you because the Lord Jesus Christ was conceived by the Holy Spirit—there is a new line of humanity. You are a part of it, if you will be.

There is a new way in his breaking with the old. He broke the traditional patterns of transmitting religion from one generation to the next, or from one person to another. Did you ever notice that before Christ, and outside of Christ, most religions in most places and times and circumstances are the religions of a tribe or a nation or a people or a race? The Hindu religion is of a certain people in India; Confucianism is of China; Islam is mostly the Arabs and their neighbors; Judaism is of the Jews. But Christianity has never been so. For most people in most places, religion was taught father and mother to son and daughter, and they to their sons and daughters on down. And that is good. The basic religious teaching must be in the home. We do far too little of it. But if it is taught solely parent to child, and that is the only way taught, then it tends to become *our* religion and *our* God, and we don't want to be so bigoted as to think that we ought to reach out and tamper with somebody else's religion or somebody else's God! Do you know, for heaven's sake, what you are saying when you say that, when you talk about "our religion" and "our God" and "their God"? You are saying this God we worship isn't God at all. The only way he can be God is to be God of everybody. Otherwise, by definition, he is not God.

Jesus Christ—from a different origin and without a human father, inspired and taught by the Holy Spirit—broke down the dividing walls of hostility. For him there was never Jew or Gentile; there was never a barbarian or a civilized person; there was never male or female; there was never a free person or a slave; there was never a Persian or a Cyrenian or an Egyptian or someone from the Hebrew nation. They were all one in Jesus Christ. We are not only free, but are commanded to go and teach and pass this good news of him who loves everybody to all people. Jesus was born of the Holy Spirit, conceived by him.

Jesus also broke with the arrogance, the unaccountable self-confidence and pride of human nature. Have you noticed that there was no initiative, no strong action on the part of the male section of the human race in the birth of Jesus? I don't want to get into an argument with anybody about whether we behave as we do as males and females because we are born that way or because we are conditioned to be that way, but I do observe that it seems to be more necessary for men than for women to do it yourself, to accomplish for yourself, and to take the initiative. It is my observation that it is often very difficult for an adult male to accept the Lord Jesus Christ and to be received into the church because there is something in this male part of the human race that says, "I can do it for myself. I can earn it for myself. I can be good enough. I can do all the good works God wants me to do. I don't need Jesus Christ. I don't need the church. I don't need grace. I don't need salvation. I can take care of myself." But when God came in human flesh, in the incarnation, when the enfleshment of God took place, the appropriate human response was uttered by Mary: "Be it unto me according as you have spoken."

And so it ever is for man or woman. When the Lord Jesus Christ, the Son of God, conceived by the Holy Ghost, born of the Virgin Mary, comes into our lives and we become a part of the new humanity—the new line of descent—we also receive him by saying, "Be it unto me according as you have spoken." This long, unbroken line of flesh and blood—father to son to son, generation to generation, hope without much progress, without destiny—went on until God broke into human flesh and started a new life.

And the domination of the thinking of men of science or otherwise was broken.

The inevitability of cause-and-effect in history was broken.

Psychological determinism of Freudianism and its tight grip upon us was broken.

The ordinary containment of religion within families and tribes and nations was broken.

And finally, the arrogance of human pride was broken, and with it the veil that hides the very face of God was broken. We see him as he is: great, awesome, majestic, but also loving us with an everlasting love.

Has it happened to you? Have you let the Holy Spirit begin to be the influence of your life? Are you becoming a part of the new line, the new humanity that begins with Jesus Christ?

Born of the Virgin Mary

Micah 7:18–20

Luke 1:46–55

*A*nd Mary said, "My soul magnifies the Lord, and my spirit rejoices in God my Savior, for he has regarded the low estate of his handmaiden."
—*Luke 1:46–48*

Born of the Virgin Mary

To advertise as one's subject "Born of the Virgin Mary" is not calculated to command instant attention. It does not startle; it does not surprise; it does not provoke; it does not intrigue. Born of the Virgin Mary: an essential part of the Christmas story, a test of orthodoxy, an article in the Apostles' Creed. This part of an affirmation of faith is a part that is frequently misunderstood, and yet it is likely that you probably think you know all about the virgin birth that you are ever going to need to know. Your being here this morning may be a real affirmation that Presbyterians do believe in worshiping God on Sunday morning, regardless.

You have heard and talked about this subject in a variety

of ways. Consequently, you have heard it and not heard it; understood it and not understood it; believed it and not believed it—all at the same time. In a word, this is one of those subjects for which you may well be inoculated and, therefore, immune.

But, suppose that we could put ourselves in the position of people who have never heard that Jesus came, born of Mary, in human flesh. Suppose we had never heard the word *incarnation* because nobody had ever needed to invent it, and suppose that the idea of the enfleshment of God was shocking and startling and new. Now, you and I cannot strap ourselves into the seat belts of a time machine and blast off for the year 1 B.C.; but we can, perhaps, look at and listen to the life of someone in our own century who has been so sealed off from believing and understanding— if not from hearing—that that person has lived out nearly a whole life, not so much in an anti-Christian state as in a pre-Christian state.

The key figure of the *Time Magazine* cover story this week was Chiang Ch'ing, the widow of Mao Tse-tung of Red China. Chiang Ch'ing was raised in terrible poverty. Her father was perhaps sixty years old when she was born, her mother perhaps forty. She had many brothers and sisters. In the interview in 1972, she never said how many. She may not have known. Her father was so cruel that he beat her mother until she finally left him. Chiang Ch'ing remembers many afternoons and nights spent simply in loneliness, waiting for her mother to come home from the poor job she had that kept them alive. She remembers one day as she was coming home from school, seeing a man carrying a pole with a dripping human head on the end of it. These were the days of so-called warlords of China.

Because of receiving a scholarship, she was able to get into acting and to move into the city, and finally to that great cosmopolitan city, Shanghai. In pre-World War II Shanghai, I understand, there was enormous wealth and privilege alongside terrible, grinding poverty and degradation. Seventy to eighty people died on the streets of Shanghai each night. Anything and anybody, it is said, could be bought and sold in Shanghai. Wouldn't that have been particularly true in the acting profession, which is hard at any age and under the best of circumstances?

Perhaps because of the lack of meaning in her life, perhaps because of miserable poverty, perhaps because of disillusionment with the corruption she saw around her, perhaps simply because nothing better was offered to her in particular, she drifted into Communism. She ended up in exile in Yenan Province after the famous Long March, met and married Mao Tse-tung, and climbed to power with him. And there she found, I suppose, along with some delights, a terrible Byzantine intrigue—a deadly, killing intrigue—with a complex cast of individuals vying for power. She became in her later years, as were those around her, a person of power, of utter ruthlessness. She enjoyed the privileges of power: the food, the palaces, the gardens, the entertainment and clothing—a lifestyle quite different from the simplicity called for in the proletarian speeches and books of her husband and herself. Nowhere in the interview is there any evidence that in this lifestyle Chiang Ch'ing found peace—certainly not any inner peace. There is no evidence of hope for anything beyond the next intrigue. There is no indication at all of joy. And as far as I can remember, the word *love* was not used.

This is the world into which Christ has not come—for all practical purposes—in human flesh. It is a dead world, a deadly world, a ruthless world, a world without meaning. And yet this is the world toward which people in Latin America and Black Africa and in other places look with hope. They see the successes of the Chinese Revolution and in many ways they want to be like them.

Can't we offer something better? Can't we show them something better? Then why don't we do it?

Jesus was born of the Virgin Mary. What does that mean?

Well, it means that in the first place, he was born. We have said it so many times in the Christmas story. Everybody who has ever heard the story of Jesus knows that he was born in a stable in Bethlehem. It means that Jesus, the Son of God, came into the world with the long, patient endurance of his mother, through the pain of his mother, and at the risk of his mother's life—as every baby is born into this world. No matter how safe we make obstetrics, a mother risks her life every time she gives birth to a child. The Son of God came humbly, with his mother giving him the great gift of life. When he came into this world his mother fed him, probably with her own milk. She bathed him. She dressed him. She changed his diapers. She carried him about as every human baby is carried about. In his first months and years he could not walk and could not talk. For the first weeks he could not focus his eyes effectively, as it is with all babies. Throughout childhood and youth he was sheltered and protected. He had to be taught a great many things, as all children and young people have to be taught. It bothers us to say that he was limited, but Jesus did not materialize like some great god from the clouds out of everywhere in general. He was born specifically in a limited geographical place, in a stable in Bethlehem. He was born in one time in the era we call the first century A.D. He was born of one specific mother, whose name we know: Mary. Jesus came literally and fully as the Son of God into human flesh. It took human flesh to get him born.

Yet he was also God. Last Sunday when we considered "Conceived by the Holy Spirit," we talked more specifically about that, but the insistence of the church that the word *Virgin* be included in "born of the Virgin Mary" is again a reminder that this was not the son of a human father. It cannot be said that Jesus was only a human being, and that later, because of his achievements, he became godly and then God; or that somehow, according to the ancient heresy, God adopted him into the Trinity. Jesus was always very much human and "Very God of Very God" at the same time. He was God who voluntarily chose to come into human flesh.

Perhaps the best way we can understand what that means is to see it from the point of view of the one who knew it first, and still has known it more intimately than anyone else who ever lived: Mary, his mother. After a bit of time to think about it and pray about it and to visit with her cousin Elizabeth, who would be the mother of John the Baptist, Mary expressed her feelings in a song of thanksgiving that we sometimes call The Magnificat. She begins this way:

My soul magnifies the Lord,
   and my spirit rejoices in God my Savior.

To magnify means if someone else is seeing God as tiny and small, I am holding up a glass with my life and with my words to show you how big he really is. To magnify God is to bubble over with the message of his greatness. She rejoiced. She magnified the Lord. Her spirit bubbles over in

. . . for he has regarded the low estate of his
   handmaiden.
For behold, henceforth all generations will call me [not
   great, but] blessed;
for he who is mighty has done great things for me,
and holy [that is, different—completely different] is his
   name.

Now this is incredible. Of course, it is a privilege for Mary to bear the Son of God. Of course, the angel came to her, and that doesn't happen to everybody. And, of course, Mary had the joy that most mothers have—of knowing that she was going to give birth. But would you have rejoiced under similar circumstances? Every one of you mothers, every teenage girl (for Mary was probably fifteen or sixteen—most Hebrew brides were), would you have rejoiced under the circumstances? To be sure, she was married, or to be married, and Joseph, a good man, a gentle man had taken her in and would not reject her. But what would happen if the family and the friends knew? Mary had had no control over the circumstances of his birth. She had no idea whether she would have any control over his life. What would it mean to bear the Son of God, to be his mother? Maybe Mary really never found out until she stood at the foot of the cross and watched him die. Mary rejoiced, incredible as it seems. The only way you can account for this is that God had come and stirred her faith. The angel had said, "Mary, I am going to use you." Mary had rejoiced at being used.

You know, that's where the joy is. That's where it always is. When these bodies, this human flesh of ours—which is ill-used, unused, misused, or used for our own purposes—is turned over so that God can use it, we find out how to live, and we rejoice in it. He had regarded the low estate of his handmaiden. He brought his Son into the world through the instrumentality of Mary's human flesh. God could use her flesh. He can use yours and mine, as lowly or as weak or as misused or as unused as it may be: God can use it.

You see, Chiang Ch'ing had been exploited and she only knew how to exploit. She had no conception of being used by God, and that makes all the difference in the world.

A few months ago, a certain woman became a grandmother for the first time. Just as she was rejoicing in this, she found herself also grieving with an older friend who had lost her husband. In the process of ministering to her daughter with the new baby and ministering to a friend in grief, she happened to come home one day with her daughter's laundry and her friend's laundry to run through her washing machine. She remarked as she brought the clean clothes back to her friend, "I thought to myself as I took my daughter's fresh new things out of the dryer and as I took your well-loved things out of the dryer, that God has time for birth and for death, and for the passing on ahead and the coming into life, and he has allowed me to have a part in both." She was happy and she made her widowed friend happy, because she felt that God was using her. That is where the joy is.

None of us want to be exploited. We will not willingly allow ourselves to be exploited by other people. We will resist it as far as we can. We do not want ourselves to be exploited by God, and we will resist him every step of the way until we are absolutely sure what kind of God this is who wants to use us.

Those thoughts must have occurred to Mary, and she touched base with her own feelings about God, for on down into the song she sang,

> . . . and his mercy is on those who fear him from
> generation to generation.

She picked up the theme again at the end:

> He has helped his servant Israel,
> in remembrance of his mercy,
> as he spoke to our fathers,
> to Abraham and to his posterity for ever.

Who is this God who wants to use us? He is the God who called Abraham out of Ur of the Chaldees to form a great nation through whom all the rest of the world would be blessed. Why? Because Abraham was good? No. Because these people would be especially good and holy?

No. It was because he chose this route to show mercy upon all the world. What kind of God is this? He is the God who called out Moses, and through Moses, the people of Israel from slavery into Egypt. Why? Because Moses was good? No. Because those folks had been nice little slaves in Egypt? No. They were even cruel to each other in some cases. He called them out because he had mercy on them and chose to have mercy through them to call the other people of the world. What kind of God is this? The God who sent his Son to become Jesus, the Christ, in human flesh, into these misused lives of ours, into this unused human flesh of ours, using Mary, who called herself "one of low degree," and then signifying that he is ready to use us.

God does use us with power. Those people in China, of whom Chiang Ch'ing is but a representative, are people who are not so much in an anti-Christian state, as they are in a pre-Christian state. There are many all over the world like them, people who cannot be used by God, partly because they have never been invited, but partly because they do not know what kind of God it is who wants to use them. Who is going to tell them? Who is going to say that Jesus was born of the Virgin Mary and came into this world to use human flesh in power?

You know, we can't give up on the Chinese. We can't give up on the Muslim Arabs, or on the Black Africans, or on the Latin Americans caught up in their intrigues and power struggles. We can't give up on the meek and the poor or on the arrogant and proud in the United States, because as Mary said, "God has shown his strength with his arm." God has, through the cross, done mighty things.

He has scattered the proud in the imaginations of their hearts. He has put down the mighty from their thrones and exalted those of low degree. He has filled the hungry with good things and the rich he has sent away empty. The cross is not now—and never has been—a symbol of defeat. It is the symbol of victory. All those nations and powerful leaders of religions and groups that have tried to stand up against Christ to defeat him have fallen down themselves in death and defeat. God really is interested in working through love and mercy, working in human flesh in strange and wonderful ways, almost always in contradiction to the power we expect to see displayed in this world.

It concerns me—though it probably doesn't concern me as often as it should and it probably doesn't concern you as often as it should—that in the Presbyterian Church we find very few of the poor and the weak. We find very few who are on welfare or who have prison records. We find very few who are slow in mentality and on the borderline of being unable to cope with the world. We find very few of those who are dirty or those who are uneducated. And yet, if God was born of the Virgin Mary, if he could recognize her low estate, if God could use her human flesh, if he can use your human flesh or my human flesh, then God is interested in and wants to use all human flesh. Because of God's desires and intentions, there is hope for the person with the prison record. There is hope for the person on welfare, even the welfare cheater. There is hope for the person who is poor and disreputable. God cares about these people. God wants to use them.

You know, there is something here about joy. Maybe some of the joylessness we experience as churchmen and as Christians is that we do not really want to take on the job of telling and showing and demonstrating and assuring and living out God's desire to use *all* human flesh—not just the human flesh we like.

This is the essence of Presbyterianism, for it is in our history and in our theology to affirm that what God is after is not just to save, but also to use. In fact, we dare not stop with talk about salvation. God—as incredible as it may sound—wants to use you, not just save you. If you want to be saved, wonderful! But don't stop there. The joy comes in being used!

Think of the joy when somehow we find the means to tell it and to show it and to demonstrate it and live it! Think of the joy when the Red Chinese come in. Think of the joy when we really begin to see something move among the Arabs, among the Muslims. Think of the joy when the revival starts in Latin America. Think of the joy in us when the poor and the weak and the uneducated and the people with prison records start coming in with us!

I am not ready to give up on any of these people, because God is not ready to give up. Jesus was born of the Virgin Mary. Jesus came in human flesh. God wants to use everybody. He won't quit until that word is heard from east to west, from north to south, from pole to pole, from New York to London, from London to Moscow, from Moscow to San Francisco, from San Francisco to Chicago, from Chicago to Atlanta, and to Marietta. He will not quit until every tongue can confess, and every knee can bow, and every human being can say that Jesus Christ is Lord, to the glory of God the Father.

God wants to use all human flesh, and to bring the joy that comes with the use. Do you trust him enough to let him use your human flesh?

Suffered under Pontius Pilate

Luke 20:1–20

S o they watched him, and sent spies, who pretended to be sincere, that they might take hold of what he said, so as to deliver him up to the authority and jurisdiction of the governor.
—*Luke 20:20*

Suffered under Pontius Pilate

Pontius Pilate strides upon the scene as a man of possessions, authority, power. He wears the purple-bordered toga of Roman authority. He is surrounded by soldiers with their burnished breastplates, their scarlet cloaks, and their plumed helmets. They are the men of the victorious legions still in the process of conquering the world. If Pilate wants something done, he has but to say the word and his command is obeyed instantly. When he goes about, he is succeeded and preceded by troops of armed and armored soldiers. He is the personal representative of Imperial Rome, appointed by the emperor himself.

Moreover, Pilate has much that seems to be desirable and enviable in the things and enjoyments of this world. If he wants food, he has but to snap his fingers. He travels about in a litter borne by slaves. He and his wife wear the latest fashions of the finest cloth that can be produced by the Roman Empire. When he is in Rome, he knows everybody who is anybody. If he wants to wash his hands, he has but to order a basin and it is brought, and another servant stands by with a towel for drying. Pontius Pilate has the power to do almost anything. No one has power exceeding his in the piece of geography called Judaea in the Roman Empire.

The Apostles' Creed tells us that the Lord Jesus suffered under this particular Pontius Pilate. That is the phrase which describes the life of Jesus. The Creed talks about birth and death. In between, there is the phrase "suffered under Pontius Pilate." There is no mention of miracles, no mention of healing, no mention of the wonderful parables of Jesus, no mention of the feeding of the five thousand or taking the children on his knee, no mention of the compassion he had on the multitudes, no mention of the transfiguration, no mention of the calling out of the apostles, no mention of the decision that had to be made when Jesus decided that he must go up to Jerusalem; only that he suffered under Pontius Pilate. And yet, when you stop and think about it, the result of every good and loving and compassionate work of Jesus was suffering for himself.

It began very early when Pilate's predecessor was ruling in Jerusalem. They excluded him from the inn. So he was born in a stable. His family misunderstood him. His neighbors in Nazareth once tried to put him to death by pushing him off a precipice. Everywhere he went, he was followed and hounded and pressed with increasing intensity by the religious rulers of his time. When he became successful, he had neither time nor place for rest. As he himself put it, "The foxes have their holes, and the birds their nests, but the Son of Man has no place to lay his head." When he insisted that he must go up to Jerusalem, he was betrayed by one friend, denied by another, seized in the night like a common thief, put on trial and condemned in the miscarriage of Roman justice and a misuse of Jewish law. He was stripped and whipped and had a crown of thorns pressed down upon his forehead and into his scalp. He was mocked and scorned and finally given the sentence of death of a common criminal. And the crowds which had before loved him so dearly and responded so enthusiastically, now in these final moments shouted, "Crucify him! Crucify him!" And the soldiers of Pilate did just that.

Now, to be sure, there were high moments of seeming victory. There were the beautiful moments when a child came and was caressed. There was the feeding of the five thousand on the rolling hills of Galilee. There were the moments when a blind man could see, and when a lame man could get up and not only walk, but run. There was the moment when a big, blustering fisherman called Peter could shout out his new insight, "You are the Christ, the Son of God!" There was that indescribable moment of the transfiguration when God himself would speak from the cloud and say, "You are my beloved Son in whom I am well pleased." But these are like little pinpricks of light, tiny stars that shine out from a panoply of darkness. For the end result of just about every good and wonderful and loving and compassionate thing that Jesus did was suffering for himself. The greater his love shown, the greater the intensity of the persecution and the pressure upon him, the more he revealed himself as he was. He suffered, yes, under Pontius Pilate.

Let us never underestimate the power of evil in that world or in our world. Let us say that Satan is powerful, but let us not blame everything upon Satan to the exclusion of ourselves. Jesus suffered under Pontius Pilate. Some of it Pilate could not have stopped because he did not know about it. Pilate could not have known how Jesus was born. He could not have known about the misunderstanding of his family. Some of it Pilate could have stopped if he had wanted to and had known about. Pilate really could not have done much about the persecution by the scribes and the Pharisees and the Sadducees. But in some of it, Pilate did the evil himself. He took the wash basin and washed his hands as though to wash the blood off beforehand. Then he took a man who he himself said was innocent and by the authority of Rome condemned him to death. He took the imprimatur of the empire and said, "This man deserves to be crucified with the worst of criminals."

So Jesus suffered physical pain and deprivation—under Pontius Pilate. He suffered the rejection and the alienation of society, and even of his close friends—under Pontius Pilate. He finally suffered the ignominy of official, authoritative condemnation, and was sentenced to death—under Pontius Pilate.

This is not what Jesus deserved, but this is exactly what sin deserves. When you and I sin against God, we deserve physical punishment. When you and I sin against God, we deserve the disapproval and rejection of our fellow human beings. When you and I sin against God, we deserve the official condemnation and sentence of death by authoritative powers. Jesus took upon himself the entire burden of sin. He took upon himself the entire guilt of sin. He took upon himself the entire package of suffering which sin calls for and deserves. And since he took the entirety of the suffering, he also worked for us the entirety of forgiveness and restoration. He took it all upon himself—all the punishment and all the hurt that we deserve—and won for us forgiveness and reconciliation to God, the freedom from sin to serve God and our fellow man, and the power to live forever.

The parable of the vineyard tells the story. Human beings want to rule the world. We think we own it. We think it is ours as did the tenants in the story. They persecuted the prophets and the spokesmen for God, and then when the Son was sent into the world, when God's very grace came in human flesh with love and compassion, the response of mankind was a loud and ugly, obscene and resounding, "No!" Jesus was made to suffer and to die. He bore it all, and because he bore it all, we and our brothers who went before who rejected him are free to accept him—freed from being victims of sin, and freed for love and service.

All the Pontius Pilates of this world seem to stride across the pages of history and of the newspapers and magazines of our lives, possessing all the power and privileges of this world. In contrast, Jesus Christ always seems to suffer and lose. How many battles of this world did he really win?

How many battles of this world does his church ever win? It never even seems to win the battle of reputation. There is always some hypocrite to belie it. Yet, today we will gather around this table as millions of other people throughout the whole world will gather around a table like it. Call it a table, call it an altar, call it Holy Communion, call it the Lord's Supper—we will gather around and remember the suffering of Jesus and the victory he won on the cross and the fact that he is alive, and we will be fed and restored and empowered thereby.

And Pontius Pilate, with his purple-bordered toga and the servants there at the snap of a finger, is remembered simply because he happened to be governor of a small piece of Roman real estate when the King of Kings suffered for us all. At first glance, Pilate is powerful and enviable. At second glance, Pilate is evil and despicable. At third glance, Pilate is like all other men—a helpless victim of sin.

Jesus, who suffered under Pontius Pilate, also suffered for all the Pontius Pilates of every age—including this one, and including you and me.

Crucified, Dead, and Buried

Psalm 16

Mark 15:21–29

*T*herefore my heart is glad, and
my soul rejoices; my body also dwells
secure. For thou dost not give me up to
Sheol, or let thy godly one see the Pit.
            —*Psalm 16:9–10*

Crucified, Dead, and Buried

Jesus set his face to go to Jerusalem. Thereafter, there was a new hardness, a steely determination about what he did and said. You can sense the judgment of God building up like a great dark thundercloud over the metropolitan center of the life of the people of God.

When he approached Jerusalem, he did not march in on horseback, followed by legions of soldiers; but he did march in as a king (albeit on a donkey), and the crowds recognized him as such and shouted their hosannas (the greeting of a king), and Jesus did not quiet them down. When he approached the temple and found it occupied by those corrupters of commerce, selling animals and exchanging money, he overturned their tables. He did this as one who has authority over the sacred places of God. A little later, when he discovered a fig tree which was not producing in season as it should, Jesus condemned it to wither. His disciples should have trembled then. Before the week was over, he was speaking in sorrow with tears in his voice regarding the destruction of this city—so holy to his people—and the fact that the temple itself, the holy place, would be demolished so that not one stone would be left standing upon another. Let there be no question about it: When Jesus came into Jerusalem in that final week, it was not simply a quiet, sweet Palm Sunday, a beautiful spring day with the birds singing and happiness everywhere.

Jesus marched into Jerusalem as the embodiment of the judgment of God upon the metropolitan center of his people's life. Consequently, when you and I repeat the Apostles' Creed, we should never trip lightly over the words "crucified, dead, and buried." It has been popular in some circles and in some places in recent years to omit the phrase "He descended into hell" from the Apostles' Creed. I doubt if the intention has been to avoid dealing with the judgment of Almighty God by omitting that phrase, but that tends to be the result. If we do not say and do not remind ourselves that when Jesus was crucified and dead and buried, he also descended into hell, then we do not remind ourselves of the magnitude of the struggle with the power of evil or the depth of the sacrifice that the Lord made on our behalf.

This week, Dr. William Muehl of the faculty of the Yale University Divinity School was speaking to the Cobb County Symposium. In the course of his address, he told this story. A woman student in the Divinity School approached him and remarked, "Dr. Muehl, I understand that you are one of those who still believe in the judgment of God." He replied, "Young lady, this is probably the only thing that I am really sure about in this life: the judgment of God." To this she responded, "How quaint!"

How quaint and how foreign to the popular thinking and the "pop" theology of our time—and even to the thinking of too many Christian people! There is the idea, and it is a popular idea, that there is no such thing as the final judgment of God—which is to say there is nobody up there who really cares one way or the other about right or wrong; or if he is up there and he does care, he doesn't bestir himself to reward or punish. People say, "Whatever I feel like doing is right, and whatever I want to do is what I should do." We call this "doing your own thing," which is a euphemism for self-indulgence and for ignoring the laws of God.

As long as there is thought to be no final judgment and that whatever feels good *is* good, then Christianity really, my friends, is irrelevant. What is the surprise of the mercy of God if there is no judgment of God? What is the point of Christ's great sacrifice to win forgiveness for us if there is no sin that is going to be condemned for which we must be forgiven? If there is no final judgment, there ultimately is no right or wrong, and there is no reward or punishment. Religion becomes a kind of an engagement in nostalgia, if you will, or according to Hugh Hefner's Playboy philosophy, a pastime for those who find it aesthetically pleasing.

Have you ever thought to yourself, or perhaps even said

aloud, "We live in a world going to hell"? The Bible uses a number of terms to designate that place, that destination of those who will not be with God for eternity in heaven. The words are *Gehenna* or *Sheol* in the Old Testament, and *Hades* or *Hell* itself, and the "nether regions beneath the earth" and the "fire prepared for the Devil and his angels" in the New Testament. But whatever the term that is used, and however hell is described, hell is that place where God is not . . . where God is not.

We live in a generation when a great many people either accidentally or deliberately have separated themselves to the extent of their power from the presence of Almighty God. They live in hell. Is it any wonder that so much of our literature concentrates upon the sad, the despairing, and the gloomy, sick behavior of people? Is it any accident that the lives of so many prominent (and not so prominent) people display the same sickness? It is the sickness of hell. They are already in it and don't know it. It touches our own lives. For such people Christ Jesus came into the world. For those who live in hell and are separated from God, Jesus was crucified, dead, and buried; he descended into hell—for that is where the problem is with so many people. That is where so many are—separated from God. Jesus went into those regions and fought the battles for them.

When Jesus came into Jerusalem there were many who knew something was astir. His disciples must have trembled and known that something of great magnitude was taking place when he overturned the tables of those who had for years done business in the temple, when the fig tree actually withered because he spoke to it, and when he predicted the destruction of the temple. But no one on the road and no one accompanying him even approached guessing that Jesus would not so much wield the judgment of God upon the city of Jerusalem as he would wield the judgment of God upon hell and Satan himself.

You know, God is patient and long-suffering, but finally he runs out of patience. As Paul tells us in the first chapter of Romans, God finally gives up and stops calling and stops summoning. He stops inviting and starts giving us over to the passions of the flesh and to the power of Satan. Jesus deliberately let himself be given to the fear of hell, to the pangs of death, to the power of Satan—on our behalf. That's the depth of the struggle. That's the magnitude of the problem. Those words, "He descended into hell," are the words that talk about where most people are. They are words that should be retained and restored and reaffirmed by Christians.

Incidentally, as we speak of "descended into hell," we Christians should remind ourselves to use words like "damn" and "hell" in their proper meaning, and be very careful not to use them lightly in expletives, lest we say to all present that it does not matter that individuals should be damned to separation from God for eternity.

How do we know that Jesus descended into hell? Well, there are verses that speak to it: the First Letter of Peter, the fourth chapter of Ephesians, the second chapter of Acts, and others. There is something more telling about the nature of Jesus' sacrifice in the Passion itself, in the time just prior to and the time when he actually died. If Jesus did not descend into hell, then what, tell me, is the greatness of the agony in the Garden of Gethsemane? Jesus prayed—not once, but several times—"Father, if it be thy will, let this cup pass from me; nevertheless, not my will, but thine be done." Luke tells us that in Jesus' agony his sweat fell onto the ground like great drops of blood. What was Jesus so troubled about? Was it the death itself? Others of far less stature than he have died serenely and bravely and with more courage displayed than Jesus seemed to be displaying—if death alone was the problem. Was it the idea of the agony of the cross? Yes, of course, that is part of it. One must never belittle the agony of dying that way, rejected by men; and yet, Jesus knew that his Father was close by and that the horror of dying would not be forever. Certainly it was not the matter of being sealed up in a tomb for a part of three days. Jesus knew that he had legions of angels at his command. No, there was something else—something else that brought on the agony, something else that called upon him to pray that the cup pass from him, something else that caused him to react physically and to sweat great drops like blood. That something else was hell. As Jesus in the Garden of Gethsemane saw it imminent, he felt disgust and revulsion at the kingdom of Satan welling up in him to the point of intense pain. He resisted it with the totality of his being.

You could say that in a psychological sense and an emotional sense Jesus began the descent into hell in the Garden of Gethsemane, for he knew then that he would be separated from God and under the power of Satan with everything he could do to torment him for a time. Then later, as he was hanging dying, holding on just to the last threads of life, the words of a psalmist who had sinned and felt himself isolated from God came into his mind and flowed out as he shouted, "Eloi, Eloi, lama sabachthani?" That is, "My God, my God, why has thou forsaken me?" And he meant just that. And he died.

I don't know much about hell. I don't know much about being damned. I don't know much about the power of Satan in any sense. But imagine or think back to the time of your worst experience of being depressed. Think of the most colossal boredom you have ever gone through for hours or even minutes. Think of your most terrible experience of being isolated, rejected, cut out, set aside from others. Think of the most intense physical pain you have ever known. Hell must be at least a hundred times worse than any of those and all of those put together. That is what Jesus took upon himself.

You and I don't really know what it is like to be isolated from God. If we just touch him now and then and feel a sense of his grace some of the time, we do not know about being isolated from God. But that's what hell is, and that's what Jesus experienced—that was the completion of the struggle. That was carrying his servanthood all the way. That was carrying love to the infinite extreme. That was doing for us what we could not do for ourselves. Jesus allowed himself to be rejected of God, turned over to Satan to receive everything that is done to one in hell, and then, and only then, to rise from the dead after Satan had done everything in his power and still could not defeat him. Because Jesus made that descent into hell, you and I are forever free from the real fears of hell. We are free from the pangs of death—that is, separation from God—and free from the power of Satan. He can never rule over our lives. This is why Jesus could say, "This is my church, and the gates of hell shall never prevail against it." Jesus went into the realms of Satan and broke down the gates of hell, that port from which the forces of evil venture out to fight and conquer the forces of good. The very gate from which they emerge has been broken down. Because Jesus went to the source, the power of Satan is forever broken in this world. You and I are free. Therefore, the continued struggle for right against wrong matters. The continued effort to find the difference between good and evil and to struggle with ethical issues, both privately and publicly, matters. That effort of ours to be responsible and faithful to God and to each other matters. Because, you see, as the cost has already been paid, and the struggle between God and Satan, between heaven and hell, between good and evil has been won, you and I are invited as free people, no longer subject to the fear or the pangs or the condemnation, to participate with Christ in the completion of his victory.

Those who waved the palm branches on the road to Jerusalem sensed something exciting. They felt something special about Jesus. Perhaps they thought he was the Son of God. Certainly the disciples (notably Peter) had thought beforehand, "This is the Son of God. This is the Christ." But the most profound observation about who Jesus was and is came from a battle-hardened Roman soldier, a centurion standing facing Jesus on the cross. Perhaps it was because this man had been in the middle of life-and-death struggles and recognized one when he saw it. Perhaps he lived in hell and knew it and wanted out. Perhaps he sensed somehow that this death was for him. I don't know. But when Jesus had said his last words, "My God, my God, why has thou forsaken me?" the Roman soldiers stood and heard, and when Jesus breathed his last and commenced his descent into hell, the centurion saw and somehow understood, and he said, "Truly this man was the Son of God." The centurion, you see, had seen men march into battle for the love of country, for the sake of honor, for the pay of a professional soldier. He had seen thousands of men risk their lives for the hope of staying alive and winning the glorious victory. He had seen the risk taken many times. But never in all his experience with battle and blood and death had he seen a man willingly and knowingly and deliberately march himself into hell for the sake of others. Only the Son of God would do that. Only the Son of God could do that.

Jesus marched into hell for you and me. Are you now willing to join with him with your life and your skills to complete the victory which he began?

Before we sing our last hymn, let us stand, and if you are willing and if you can say the words with conviction, let us say again in affirmation of our faith the Apostles' Creed, and let us include in its appropriate place the words "He descended into hell."

I believe in God the Father Almighty, Maker of heaven and earth; and in Jesus Christ His only Son our Lord; who was conceived by the Holy Ghost, born of the Virgin Mary, suffered under Pontius Pilate, was crucified, dead, and buried; He descended into hell; the third day He rose again from the dead; He ascended into heaven, and sitteth on the right hand of God the Father Almighty; from thence He shall come to judge the quick and the dead. I believe in the Holy Ghost; the holy Catholic Church; the communion of saints; the forgiveness of sins; the resurrection of the body; and the life everlasting.

Amen.

He Rose from the Dead

Isaiah 64

Matthew 27:55; 28:1–20

So they departed quickly from the tomb with fear and great joy, and ran to tell his disciples.

—Matthew 28:8

He Rose from the Dead

It is cool and still and very, very dark in the hour just before dawn. The blackness gives way first to a kind of grayness. Even if there are no mists of morning, the gray comes before the warmer colors of sunrise. If one had a proclivity to believe in ghosts or disembodied spirits, this would be the time when he would expect them to appear. Even practical, sober, down-to-earth people who do not believe in such things do not visit the cemetery by choice in the gray, ghostly time just prior to dawn.

Why would Mary and her friends go? Perhaps it was the result of yet another sleepless night. Perhaps they were still numb and in shock from grief. There they were, without escort and without real purpose except the sad business of anointing from their tiny bottles of ointment and spices, descending into the valley of the dead where for many generations the limestone cliffs had been carved into sepulchers.

They drew close, identified the sepulcher, and saw the soldiers standing guard. Then there was a kind of roaring sound that got louder and louder. The leaves on the trees began to agitate, though there was no wind. The earth began to shake beneath their feet. Those who have been in earthquakes say that they last but seconds, but are enough to drive you insane because everything you have ever depended upon moves and will not be still. Mary and her friends and the soldiers were picked up and tossed down on the ground as if by a giant's hand. Then as they opened their eyes and looked up, there was a dazzling sight. The stone that had sealed the sepulcher had been moved in the earthquake. Sitting upon the stone was someone who looked like a man and yet was not a man. His visage was so dazzling it was like lightning. His garment was so white it glistened like snow. This was enough for the soldiers. They fell down as men who were dead—paralyzed, unconscious. Mary Magdalene, Mary, the mother of James and John, and the other Mary were somehow able to look. They heard the angel say, "Do not be afraid; for I know that you seek Jesus who was crucified. He is not here; for he has risen, as he said." They could feel the joy beginning to rise up. They hardly dared believe what he was saying.

Then after he had told them to go to Galilee and they started off to tell the disciples, there was Jesus. "Hail."

In another version, the first word Jesus spoke was "Mary."

The Scripture tells us that the response of these human beings who were present reflected two of the most powerful emotions known to human beings: fear and joy. One of the best pieces of evidence that Jesus really rose from the dead is the confusion in the reports about his resurrection. You know, if you conspire to invent a story, you rehearse, you get your story straight, and you tell it correctly in every detail. But when something true has happened and many witnesses see it, and particularly if it is an event of intense emotional impact, all of the witnesses will remember the details in slightly different fashion. They tell what they saw, but two human beings do not see the same event the same way. If you read Matthew, Mark, Luke, and John, and then Paul's partial account of the resurrection, you have five different stories to some degree, but they all testify to the overwhelming nature of the event, and that fear was present and that joy was present.

It was appropriately so, and it still is. It is appropriate that you and I on this given Easter Sunday, or on any Easter Sunday, should respond to the retelling of the events of Easter first with fear, then with joy—and then, with a combination of fear and joy.

Let us look at the fear first. All it took was the combination of the grayness just before dawn, the shaking of the earth, and the appearance of the angel, and the soldiers fell down like dead men, unconscious. They knew what was going on. These men could well have been in the contingent that went out to arrest Jesus in the Garden of Gethsemane. They could have been a part of those groups that dragged him from the Sanhedrin to the courtyard of Pilate, to the palace of Herod, back to Pilate's courtyard, and then turned him over to the Roman soldiers to be scourged and then crucified. They knew that the authorities thought he was a troublemaker. They also knew he had been illegally arrested, unfairly tried, and then put to death. He was crucified, dead, and buried. They were ordered to see that he remained dead and buried. They were standing guard over his tomb lest his disciples steal his body.

Men had done everything they could, and then it went haywire. Men lost control. Suddenly the earth shook. You can't stop that. Suddenly the stone they had so carefully rolled into place (and it took many of them to do it) had rolled away on its own. Suddenly there was some kind of extra-human being out there with a shining visage. It was more than the conscious mind could take, and they fainted.

Now, it is important that you and I feel something of the fear of that morning. It is important that you and I get some sense of the need for trembling on Easter Sunday. A great wrong was done and God righted the wrong. God can and will do it again. God made human eyes focus on a being such as those human eyes had never seen before. God could do it again to you or to me or to anyone else. God so charged that atmosphere with power that men and women literally could not stand, and God can do it again. Let me tell you something: Jesus did not slip gently back into life as you and I would stroll from store to store in Cumberland Mall on a Saturday afternoon in April. Jesus roared back into life with power, accompanied by an earthquake.

Look at yourself. Look at what you do to other people.

Look at what you don't do *for* other people. Look at all the events of your life in which you ignore the Lord God, and all those hours of your day when you forget that he even exists. Remember that God can roar into our life with resurrecting power as he roared into that first Easter Sunday morning and raised Jesus from the dead. It is appropriate that we should be afraid. It is appropriate that there should first be trembling on Easter Sunday morning. Something powerful is afoot here. We need to know that.

But fear by itself will not do, for fear does not produce life, and it certainly does not produce the Christian life. The first thing it produces is what it produced in those soldiers: paralysis. They dropped as dead men and did nothing. Then when they began to get feeling in hands and feet, and to recover their eyesight, they did worse than nothing. They set out to get false rumors spread around so that they would protect themselves from being punished or spoken against. Think of the absurdity of it! The Son of God has been raised from the dead. These are among the first witnesses to the most momentous event in human history (and they had some notion of what was going on, as we all do) and they set about first off to take care of what somebody else might be saying about them, instead of spreading the word of the resurrection.

Actually, it is not so absurd, is it? It is not so foreign, either. There are people in your neighborhood and in your school and in your business and close to you in your profession who are living in hell right now. And there are people around you who are waking up to the glory and wonder of God and to the new life he offers in his Son.

Look at the time you and I waste worrying about what somebody is thinking about what we are doing. That's what fear does to you. Fear by itself is not enough.

And then, there was joy. Mary and her friends must have sensed that something was going to happen that morning. Even as the earth began to be unstable and to shake beneath their feet and they could see the stone moving, they knew from what grave that stone was moving. And I think they recognized an angel when they saw one; and when the first words came, "Be not afraid," they began to sense the joy. They began to anticipate what would be next. And when Jesus came and greeted them, and then began to speak their names, they fell down on their faces and caught hold of his feet and worshiped him. This had never happened before. You see, the disciples had speculated that Jesus just might be the Son of God. Peter and perhaps one or two others had said it aloud. But now it was absolutely certain. This Jesus who had been crucified, dead, and buried, was alive. They were sure now that he was the Son of God, in human flesh, alive and standing before them.

Don't you see? That makes everything new. Everything starts all over. For all the political forces of the time had been gathered. They had done to Jesus what they could. All the religious and civil forces of that time had been gathered together. They did what they could to Jesus: crucified him and put him to death. The people gathered and shouted, "Crucify him! Crucify him!" They begged for Barabbas, the murderer, to be released to them instead of Jesus. They did what they could, and Jesus still did not stay dead. After government authority, after religious authority, and after mob rule had done their worst, Jesus rose and made all things new. For, you see, no human power can control the power of the risen Christ. God and good have won and will win—not only out there in the world, in your office, in your school, in your neighborhood, where you work and where you live, but also God and good have won and are winning inside you. Evil will not triumph. You shall be better than you are because Christ is alive and in you. There is the joy.

But let us always see the joy and the fear together, lest what we think be joy be only froth, something worthless and soon gone.

You and I have stood many times in a football stadium—at Sanford Stadium or at Grant Field or Northcutt Stadium or wherever—and have wanted the team to win so badly. You have jumped up and down and you have clapped your hands and you have yelled yourself hoarse. You have argued verbally with the officials though they could not hear you. You identified fully with the struggle. And then, at last, you won. The elation and the joy last a few minutes, maybe a few hours. But life goes on. Even if you played in the game—and, oh, it is sweeter to win than it is to lose—still life goes on. So it is with all the games of life, whether they have to do with sports or making money or social occasions or school or whatever. The joy from human events does not last. What you and I need when we walk away from church on Easter Sunday morning is the same kind of double feeling with which Mary and her friends walked away from the first Easter experience. They walked away shaken by the fear and overwhelmed by the joy.

If you can take the fear and the joy in combination, then you can begin to know that strange, abundant life where you know who is in control of these frightening events and of your life. You can begin to trust that same person to control the future.

That is what made the difference. Mary and her friends were first afraid, and then they understood who it was that was in control of these events that shook them so badly, and that made all the difference in the world.

A few years ago, I was on the staff of the Board of Christian Education of our church, then in Richmond, Virginia. There were over two hundred persons employed by that board. Not very large as corporations go, but the influence of that board spread across our whole church and across many denominations. There was considerable power wielded, a good bit of money spent, a diversity of services rendered, and many opportunities for mistakes. But Dr. Marshall Dendy was executive secretary of that board. As long as Dr. Dendy was there, you knew that mistakes would not be allowed to lie untended for long. They would be corrected. You knew that no one would be treated unfairly or ungraciously. Now, if you have taught in a good school system with a strong superintendent, if you have been an employee of a good firm with a strong president, if you have been in any kind of situation where somebody at the top was strong and good, you know what I am talking about. There is fear of the authority, but joy that it is being done right.

That's what Mary—ten times, twenty times, a hundred times more—felt that Easter Sunday morning. The events were overwhelming. Any intelligent human being would be afraid. But look who was in control of the events! Joy and fear are combined. When these two are combined, there also begins to tug at you the desire to be a part of it yourself. When you sense that God Almighty is acting and doing and working and accomplishing something, and that this is where the power is, this is where the action is, you want to be there, too. In fact, you become more afraid of being left out than you are afraid of participating.

I remember only too well a Senior High Work Camp over in Birmingham Presbytery some seven, eight, nine years ago now. It was at the beginning of operating a newly constructed presbytery camp. The work was hard and hot and difficult and sometimes the young people were a little afraid of getting up in the morning and facing it. But the week progressed. They began to sense that God was allowing them to do something important for somebody else. There was a kind of joy on those sweaty faces— all except for Martha's. I have to tell you about Martha. I had divided the camp into four or five work groups. They were doing a variety of different jobs and working in different parts of the camp. So I told them, "Don't listen for a bell to take a break at ten or eleven o'clock in the morning. Take a break as groups whenever you are tired and you need one." That was Martha's opportunity. I began to go about the camp and to check on the progress of each group. Everywhere I found a group resting, I also found Martha. Martha rested with every group, all day and all week. And you know, the sad thing is that Martha never knew the joy of what they were doing. She had no fear of me as the director. But because she rested with every group, she never knew the joy of what was happening, either. Put fear and joy together, and it just demands your participation.

Jesus said, "All authority in heaven and on earth is given to me. Go, therefore, and make disciples of all nations, baptizing them in the name of the Father and of the Son, and of the Holy Spirit, and teach them everything that I have commanded you." Recognize the power. Experience the joy. Participate.

When love and joy are combined, you know what the future will be like. When you take the joy and fear and add them up, put them on a line like an algebraic equation, the sum that you get is love. It is almost as if you could say that fear plus joy equals love. For the message of the earthquake, the message of the empty tomb, the message of the presence of the angel, the message of the situation charged with power is this: the power is for you. It is God's love in action—in powerfully charged action. Jesus said, "Lo, I am with you always."

Let us go back now for a moment to that gray hour just before dawn. Let the earth shake beneath your feet. Let the stone be rolled away before your eyes. Let the tomb be seen as empty. Let there be an angel sitting there saying, "Be not afraid." Let yourself feel the power—the power that is for you. There is fear and there is joy. Because there was both fear and joy, it is light now. And it will never be dark again.

He Ascended into Heaven

Psalm 68:1–20

Acts 1:1–11

And while they were gazing into heaven as he went, behold, two men stood by them in white robes, and said, "Men of Galilee, why do you stand looking into heaven? This Jesus, who was taken up from you into heaven, will come in the same way as you saw him go into heaven."

—Acts 1:10–11

He Ascended into Heaven

I suppose that it is possible to grow accustomed even to resurrection. I suppose that one could in time get used to the company of someone who had been raised from the dead. But when Jesus was first risen, the disciples were awed into silence. They fell down and worshiped him. Thomas, who had said, "I will not believe until I poke my fingers into the nail prints and thrust my hand in his side where the sword went," could say nothing more than, "My Lord and my God," when he did see Jesus.

But time passes. There were forty days and nights in which Jesus appeared and reappeared to his disciples. One would not exactly say that they grew restless, but one could say that they were beginning to sense that something else was supposed to happen. Something had been completed and something else needed to start. On this particular occasion, several of them summoned courage and approached Jesus when he was with them. They must have given this kind of preface: "Lord, we know that you are the Messiah, the one who was promised. We know you are the Christ, the Son of the living God. We know that you are raised from the dead." Then they asked, "But are you going to restore the kingdom of Israel at this time?"

It would seem that was Jesus' signal. It was the sign that his work was done.

He did not answer them directly. He never answered directly questions about times and seasons. He always said, "It is not for you to know." But he did say, "You shall be my witnesses, and you shall receive power."

At that moment he was taken away—not by death, not by any action of human beings, but by the power of God. He was lifted off the face of the earth and he disappeared into the clouds. While the disciples still did not know what was happening, while they were still looking off up yonder at the spot in the heavens at which he was last seen, there appeared two men like angels, dressed in white, there alongside them asking, "You men of Galilee, why are you standing here looking off up into the sky? This Jesus who has been taken from you will return in the same way that you saw him go. Why are you standing here?"

That question had never been asked of Jesus' disciples before. It demonstrates a change in God's expectations regarding these men who had been so close to Jesus. Up until now it had been all right to stand still, to watch and listen. When Jesus had preached and taught in Galilee, it was the role of the disciples to stand by and watch and listen. When Jesus had his disputations with the scribes and Pharisees, he had never insisted that they join in and embroil themselves, but rather they had stood and listened. When Jesus prayed in agony in the Garden of Gethsemane, all he expected from the disciples, as he stated, was that they should watch and pray. As he was hanging on the cross dying, the disciples watched from afar and no one questioned their watching. Even when Jesus had risen from the dead, when he appeared to them in the upper room and in other places, mostly the disciples watched and listened, and there was no quarrel with their watching and listening. Up until this point, they had been disciples, those who are under the discipline of learning.

In this moment when Jesus ascended into heaven, they became apostles. Pending the action of the Holy Spirit, they would be the church. God's expectations had at this moment changed. When Jesus' work on the cross and in the resurrection in revealing God and working salvation was completed and he was taken up into heaven, the disciples' work was to begin. They were to become not disciples: those who were learning; but apostles: those who were sent to do something.

You and I, like most modern-day Christians, tend to satisfy ourselves with standing and looking up at the sky. It is good to listen to sermons and to be made to think by them. We must continue to do it. It is good to be in a church school class and to discuss the meaning of what God has done and is doing. We must continue to do it. It is good to pray and to meditate about what God is about in this world. It is good to sit on the bank of a lake or to

sit on a mountaintop and look up at the stars and to con-
template the nature of the deity who made us and what he
is doing. It is good to ask the questions of yourself, as the
disciples asked themselves, "Do you understand? Do you
believe?" But now there comes a third question: "Why are
you standing here looking up at the sky?"

Let us take a few moments to look more closely at what
occurred when that third question was asked, so that we
who also are close to Jesus may understand what is meant
when the third question is asked of us.

When Jesus ascended into heaven, there was a coinci-
dence of the grace of God and the omnipotent power of
God. Jesus prayed, as John records it, that he might be
allowed to share the glory with the Father which they
shared from the foundation of the world. Paul wrote in
the Letter to the Ephesians that when Jesus ascended into
heaven, he would "fill all things," or "fulfill all things," or
"complete all things." It was the theologian Karl Barth
who used this particular language. When Jesus ascended
into heaven, "at long last grace and omnipotence could be
seen to be one and the same." The Old Testament had
understood the omnipotent power of God without question. The Old Testament saw God as the one who was
high and lifted up in Isaiah's vision, whose train filled the
temple, who filled it with smoke, who caused the foundations of the threshold to shake. This was the God who
could divide the Red Sea and destroy Pharaoh's army. This
was the God who could cut a covenant with Moses, cut
into the rock of Mount Sinai. This was the God who could
destroy Sodom and Gomorrah, the God who could oblit-
erate those who worshiped the golden calf. This was the

God who could take the tramping soldiers of Cyrus the Persian with their bloodthirsty motives and use them in order to punish the Babylonians. The Old Testament understood omnipotence—all power belonging to God—and the exercise of it. That is one picture, the picture of power.

When God came in human flesh, another picture was seen: Jesus sitting and taking one child after another upon his lap, resting his hand upon each head, gazing intensely into each individual pair of eyes, speaking a unique blessing for each potential adult, and then commenting to those who stood by, "Of such is the kingdom of heaven." There is also another part to that same picture: Jesus taking his hand and reaching down into the dust and pulling upright a woman who had been caught in the act of adultery and who was almost stoned, forgiving her, and then saying, "Go and sin no more." Most poignantly, the picture includes Jesus' hands and feet nailed to the cross, the soldiers taking that cross and then lifting it up and then dropping it down with a heavy and agonizing thud into the ground, and Jesus, not crying out in pain, not cursing in bitterness, but speaking the first words of the crucified, "Father, forgive them, for they know not what they do." That is the other picture: the picture of grace.

When Jesus ascended into heaven, the picture of the omnipotence of God in the Old Testament and the picture of the grace of God in the New Testament are merged into one. Grace sits enthroned, and is expressed in omnipotent power. Do you believe that? Then why are you standing here looking at the sky?

There is something else. You will notice as we repeat

the words of the Apostles' Creed, that when we come to this point, the tense changes from past to present. Listen to the verbs, how they look back and recite the history of what God has already done in the past in Jesus Christ: *conceived* by the Holy Ghost, *born* of the Virgin Mary, *suffered* under Pontius Pilate, *crucified, dead,* and *buried; descended* into hell; *rose* again on the third day; *ascended* into heaven. . . . And then it changes from past to present: *sitteth* on the right hand of God the Father Almighty. He *sits* there. It's *now;* it is *not then.* It is not something that has gone by and is to be told about in a history book. This is what *is.* Grace and omnipotence are together *now.*

This is the power that rules the world. Are there wars and rumors of wars? Is there disintegration of family life? Is there more violence and misuse of sex? Are there more crimes than there used to be? Does it seem that there are more tornadoes, earthquakes, and occasions of drought than before? That's not the final word! The final word is that the God of grace is the God who rules and the God who rules is a gracious God. The power that sustains the power of earthquakes and tornadoes and all the activities (good and bad) of men, is a power that is not against us, but for us. You and I can look disaster and death itself in the face with confidence, because Jesus has ascended into heaven. Do you believe that? Then why are you standing here looking up at the sky?

There is something here to be told. There is a message here that must be told. There is a power for the telling of it. Jesus said, "You shall receive power when the Holy Ghost has come upon you." He said, "All authority in heaven and earth is given to me; therefore, go ye into all the world and make disciples of all nations." The Great Commission, the foundation for the missionary activity of the church, is in the ascension of Jesus Christ to sit on the right hand of God the Father Almighty. For, you see, the right hand is the place from which power is dispensed. It is the place of the prime minister, the first counselor of the realm in a kingdom. When Jesus sits there, by the wonderful and incredible grace of God, you and I sit there with him.

Barth points out that the incarnation (the coming in human flesh) and the crucifixion of Jesus are the humiliation of God. This is what Jesus did for us and to reveal God to us. But the ascension into heaven is the exaltation of man. Jesus came down that he might take us up with him, so that when you and I do the actions of God and speak the things that God wants spoken, we do it with the very power of God. Did you notice that the Great Commission given in Matthew is given with authority and power? "All power in heaven and earth is given to me. Go therefore . . . and lo, I am with you always." "I," being Jesus, is the one who has the gracious power. Jesus says here, as recorded in Acts, "You shall receive power when the Holy Spirit is come upon you, and you shall be my witnesses." There is a kind of inner urgency that we must speak, we must tell what God is doing, we must tell about the grace, we must tell about the power, we must tell about what Jesus did, but we also must tell about who rules *now*.

In this last week our president has been talking about an energy crisis. I suspect he is right. No one knows the details of the future; but in general, what he has been saying are things we need to know and things we need to think about and need to prepare for. I have no doubt but that there will be sacrifices that must be made. There will be some suffering. Certainly there will be changes, and it is a time to begin to look at those things. But we who are close to Jesus know—as the world does not—that this is not a time for depression. This is not a time for despair. This is not a time for panic. God, who is the God of grace and of glory, the God of love and power, is the one who reigns. In spite of all that is said, man does not live by oil alone, or by coal alone, any more than he lives by bread alone. If all the oil is poured out tomorrow, and all the coal is burned up tonight, you and I will survive and we will triumph. We will still have power with which to live and to change the world, for God is not only the creator of all the sources of energy, he is above all the sources of energy. He can and will work to do with us beyond our imagining, regardless of the circumstances.

Don't you see that the good news of Jesus Christ is the good news that must be told in an oil crisis, if that is where we are? It must be told in the midst of hunger, if that is where we are. It must be told when a death has come or when your personal life seems to be disintegrating, if that is where you are. If it is not a gospel for all the circumstances of life, it is no gospel at all. It is that, and it is something that has an inner urgency about it. It must be told, and we must do the telling. Do you believe that? Then why are you sitting here looking up at the sky?

There is also an outer urgency about the telling. When Jesus ascended into heaven, his work as Jesus of Nazareth—as God incarnate in human flesh—was done. He returned to the Father, and the disciples' work began. Those who had been under the discipline of learning became apostles—those who were sent out. The era of the church began. The time of the church is the time of God's patience. It is the time when the telling must be done. That's why we are here, friends—to tell what we know. That's why we are here—to make it known. That's the purpose of the church—to reveal this God of grace and God of glory (in Fosdick's hymn), this God of love and omnipotent power—power and love that apply to the specific situations of right now. The church has not always existed. The church will not always exist. It will be here for God's good time and then no more. All the telling must be done in that time.

Last summer, so I am told, nine or ten inches of rain fell in one night over Estes Park in Colorado. Before the early evening had come, the reservoir had been filled and topped. A wall of water some say to have been thirty to forty feet high came rolling down the canyon of the Big Thompson River where hundreds of people were camped in tents, campers, and cabins—fishing and simply enjoying the wonder of the Rocky Mountains. As that wall of water began its way down the canyon, a certain deputy sheriff in Fort Collins, Colorado, at the mouth of the canyon, heard the word on the radio of a terrible flood. He had a choice: he could stay in Fort Collins and be safe himself, or he could take the chance of driving up into the Big Thompson Canyon as far as he could go to wake and warn as many people as possible. He chose to go and tell. He lost his car; he spent many hours on a rock ledge; he almost lost his life. But there are people alive today because that deputy sheriff chose to go and tell them while there was still time.

Jesus Christ has ascended into heaven. The grace of Jesus who took children on his lap and forgave those who crucified him has been merged into the omnipotent power revealed in the Old Testament. That is the power which rules—not just yesterday, but now and forever. There is an outward urgency in this time of God's patience that the telling be done.

You have often heard the questions in one way or another. Do you understand? Do you believe? Do you now hear a third question? It goes something like this: Why are you standing here looking up at the sky?

He Shall Come to Judge the Quick and the Dead

Ezekiel 34:11–24

Matthew 25:31–46

*T*hen the King will say to those at his right hand, "Come, O blessed of my Father, inherit the kingdom prepared for you from the foundation of the world."

—*Matthew 25:34*

He Shall Come to Judge the Quick and the Dead

When my mother was a little girl, she had an Aunt Lolly who lived with the family. I guess that in the days of larger houses and no nursing homes, everybody had an "Aunt Lolly"—an elderly aunt or other person who had more time than the other adults to spend with children. When my mother wished that she could have something, and perhaps cried because she could not, Aunt Lolly would say, "I'll get you one when my ship comes in." Now, everybody knew that Aunt Lolly didn't have a ship, but her hopefulness was enough to help a little girl get over her disappointment.

I wonder where we got that phrase, "When my ship comes in." Does it come out of the pre-Civil War South?

The bales of cotton from the plantations were floated down the river at New Orleans or Savannah and then shipped to England. Payment for the crop was received when the ship came back months later. So one waited for one's ship to come in? Or is this an item out of the sailing days of New England? One voyage to the Orient for trading could make the family that owned the ship wealthy. To be sure, it was risky. Sometimes the ships and all the hands were lost at sea, but there were fortunes to be made "when my ship comes in." Waiting for a ship with eager expectations could get one through some awfully hard New England winters.

We all need to have hope. We all need to have confident expectations about the future. We all need to believe that tomorrow or the day after tomorrow, or at the very least next week, will be better than today. If you are a college student, you need to believe in the day after the last exam.

But there are not very many treasure ships out there any more, are there? In the U.S.A. it is not common to live with high hopes. Perhaps it is because we lost the war in Vietnam. We no longer can really believe in the absolute perfection and the absolute successfulness of the U.S.A. in every venture.

We no longer believe that we can do whatever we want to with this planet of ours. We can no longer pollute its air and pollute its water and use up all of its burnable resources and cover the surface of it with asphalt and concrete and still be able to enjoy the use of it forever. That clouds the future a bit, doesn't it?

Perhaps we have grown discouraged and despairing because of what we see happening to family life and to morals in this country. Unless we do some planning and act carefully now, the future may look bleak indeed.

Perhaps it is because there is no more frontier. That big West out there used to be vast enough to forgive almost anything, and broad enough to provide the space for a new life in the future. But there isn't any frontier anymore. How do you look for hope in the future if you have disappointment in the present?

Next month I will have been an ordained minister for twenty years. Never in those years do I remember a time when there seemed to be in the society abroad more of a hunger to know if there is some word from God. To be sure, the church has been stating that word all along. Perhaps it is preparing itself to say it more clearly now. At least we know some of the answers that are not very helpful.

In the mid-sixties and in the early seventies, many Christians—out of genuine Christian commitment—responded to those passages of the Bible that say we must feed the hungry and clothe the naked and give drink to the thirsty and visit the prisoners and all the rest. They set out through political and social action to create the perfect society. Maybe it was because technology had brought us to the point that it seemed at least possible that we could meet everybody's physical needs. But they reckoned without the perplexity and the perversity of human nature, didn't they? We could call it by the plain and ugly word *sin*. Somehow the bright new day that a great many people worked for and hoped for has not dawned, in spite of all the Christian commitment and genuine Christian concern.

During the same period, we began to hear the despairing voices of those who now wanted to predict gloom and doom. They published their books like *The Late Great Planet Earth*. They involved themselves in all the intricacies of the "Old Dispensationalism" and the "New Dispensationalism," and began to do what I call "playing around with prophecy" in the Bible. And yet, the predicted doom has not come, either. Nothing gets quite so boring or useless as the catastrophe that never arrives. Besides, it is unbecoming and probably faithless for Christians to be in paralyzing despair because a part of the world they live in has grown sour. Our Lord himself said it is more our business to give love to our neighbors than to predict the future. There are still needs to be met, and there is help we can render.

We do need hope. But what we need to do is to not be distracted by obscure prophecies nor to pretend that sin is not very powerful. Rather, we need to take sin seriously, and we need to take to heart the very clear promises—not the prophecies, but the promises—given in the Scripture.

The Creed reminds us that Jesus "sitteth on the right hand of God the Father Almighty; from thence he shall come to judge the quick and the dead."

Several passages of Scripture are pulled together and summarized in this one article of faith expressed in the Creed. The one that is the most comprehensive and is at the same time the most clear (or so it seems to me), is this twenty-fifth chapter of the Gospel of Matthew—Jesus' vision of the separation of the sheep and the goats. It is familiar, so I will not try to paint again the picture of the final judgment as it is given here.

I would like to do two things. The first is to call to your

attention the basic elements involved in Jesus' coming again. The second is to point out what we can learn that can feed our hopes for the future.

First of all, Jesus will come again. Jesus pointed to "when the Son of man comes in his glory." ("Son of man" was Jesus' favorite term for himself.) There is no doubt about who is intended here. John recalls that Jesus said, "If I go, I will come again, and receive you unto myself." When Jesus was taken up into the clouds into heaven, the angel who stood by the apostles said that this Jesus who had ascended will descend in a way as unexpected as he was taken from them. In writing to the church at Thessalonica, Paul said, "He will descend from the heavens and the dead will be raised." At the very end of the Bible, the Book of Revelation—after it talks about judgment here and judgment there—finally comes to a thunderous crescendo of triumph: the Lamb (that is, Jesus) who was slain will return and claim his own, and they shall reign for ever and ever. Nothing in Scripture is really clearer—nothing other than God's love—than the promise that Jesus will come again.

The second element is that the one who comes again is the same Jesus who came before. Now, that should be obvious; but it is very important that we know that. When I was a little boy and my teachers in Sunday School talked about Jesus, I could respond warmly and readily when they talked about his taking little children on his knee. I could respond readily when they talked about his helping a man who was lame to be able to walk. I could respond to his giving sight to the blind. I could even respond to the ugly picture of Jesus being crucified, as soon as I understood that he loved us that much. But something happened when teachers began to talk about Jesus coming again. You Sunday School teachers take note here. I wonder if there was a change in the tone of voice with which the teachers talked about this. I wonder if the teacher was afraid of the Second Coming, or wasn't quite sure whether it was really the same Jesus. But anyway, when the teacher talked about his coming again, I got scared, and I didn't like any part of that. Let me tell you something. If you can believe that Jesus would have loved you if you had been there in Galilee when he taught and healed, then also believe that he will love you when he comes again. It's the same Jesus.

The third element is that this time he will come with unmistakable power. This time when he comes, there will be no cross. This time when he comes, there will be no defeat. This time when he comes, there will be no uncertainty. This time when he comes, love will triumph universally, obviously, and finally.

Then, the fourth element is that there is going to be a judgment. What the Bible means by judgment, as we really do when we think about it, is a separation. Jesus said that when the Son of man comes in all his glory, when he sits on this glorious throne and all his angels are around him, then he will call all nations to him and he will separate the sheep from the goats. You remember the parable he told about the wheat and the tares (or weeds). Someone asked the landowner, "Do you want us to go and pull the weeds?" He said, "No, you will pull up the sprouts of wheat. Wait until the harvest, when it is all cut down. Then separate the wheat from the tares." There will be that one great separation when the sons of God will be revealed. There will be that day, as Paul said, "toward which all creation groans, when the sons of God will be revealed." For them to be revealed, they will have to be separated from all the others. There will be a judgment, when a decision is made about who belongs to God and who does not; who is saved and who is not; who is a sheep and who is a goat; who is on the right hand and who is on the left hand. There will be a judgment.

And the next element is that that judgment will be for all nations. I can't give you a schedule. I can't tell you who comes in what order. I can't tell you who has the highest priority. But it will be judgment for the good and the evil. It will be judgment for Christian and for Jew. It will be judgment for those who are living and for those who are dead. Paul says in one place, "The living will be changed. The souls of the dead will be rejoined with their bodies, and all will be caught up together in the air." There are all sorts of obscure prophecies about the first resurrection and the second resurrection and the lake of fire and the great white throne. There are some who figure out of Revelation somehow that there is going to be a separate destiny for Jews and for Christians. My Bible reads that there is one gospel and one judgment for all. It seems to me it is much better for us to follow that which is plain and clear than to get ourselves involved in all sorts of obscure prophecies that distract us from the gospel and from what the Scripture plainly teaches. So one judgment will be for all people. That judgment will be based on the criterion of the way we do the acts of love.

I was hungry and you gave me food; I was thirsty and you gave me drink; I was a stranger and you welcomed me; I was naked and you clothed me; I was sick and in prison, and you visited me.

We will be judged on the way we treat each other—our neighbors. Jesus identified himself with our neighbors. Thus, the criterion is our loving acts towards our neighbors and our loving acts towards God. The Great Commandment: "You shall love the Lord your God with all your heart, and with all your soul, and with all your mind, and with all your strength. And the second is like unto it: You shall love your neighbor as yourself." That is what Jesus commanded. That is the basis upon which we will be judged finally.

And then—and this is the last one—there will be reward and there will be punishment. Just because God's love will triumph does not mean that the evil will get the same recompense from God as the good. I don't know what hell is like. I don't know what its furnishings look like. I don't know what its temperature is. I don't know what its dominant colors are. But the Bible says throughout that there is a place, or there is a residence, or there is a state of being that is separated from God. Now, it is probably not down under the earth. We are not caught up in geography here. It may not be in any particular level of the clouds. It is probably in a dimension, as heaven is, that we do not know anything about in this life. Nevertheless, it is sometimes called "hell"; it is sometimes called "Hades"; it is sometimes called "Sheol." It is the place of the dead where God is not.

Archbishop William Temple of Canterbury once remarked that if there were no hell, there ought to be one for those who want to go there. Its chief characteristic is torment, which is another way of saying separation from God and love. The tragic thing is that there are a lot of people who live in torment because they are separated from God and they really don't know there is anything better. This punishment is self-imposed. These people choose God's presence or his absence for themselves. Those who want to live in the presence of God will get their desire. Those who do not want to live in the presence of God will get their wish for eternity. There is reward, and there is punishment.

Now what can we learn from all of this? Well, first of all, that there is meaning and purpose in life. Jesus is coming again. He is going to complete what he started. It is all going to be put together and finished. There is meaning and purpose in your life and in my life and in the whole history of the world.

When I read a novel, I like for it to have a beginning, a middle, and an end. I like for something to be changed or something to be moved or something to happen. I like for the good guys to win and the bad guys to lose. When people now write novels or television programs or movies, they tell you what their philosophies are. Don't let yourself be kidded. When the writers continually throw at you that which is degrading and despairing, they are not telling you the truth about what the world is like. They are telling you the truth about what their souls are like. You don't have to let them provide the content for yours as well.

Jesus is coming again. That's what we focus on. That good and that righteousness and that wholeness and that love which we are called to live—that is what will be completed and fulfilled, even if it is not obvious to you now.

About two years ago, we began to build our new building, Holland Hall, behind this sanctuary. The first thing we did was to have the demolition workers come in and tear down the old. At one point if you had driven up to the parking lot and looked back there, you might have supposed that a tornado, a fire, or an explosion had done its work. But if you knew the plan and the promise, you also knew that that which we had at last begun was a sign of hope. If you know what God has promised—that Christ will come again, the same Christ will come again—then you know that life has meaning, and that it is going somewhere with God's purposes.

The second thing we learn from all of this is that this is a moral universe. The righteous will be rewarded and the evil will be punished. Have you ever said to yourself when you heard about something particularly cruel or vicious, "There must be a special place in hell reserved for people who do such things"? Of course. You are right. That's what happens to people who do such things unless that process in life is reversed by repentance. This is a moral universe.

Now, it is not very becoming and it is not very helpful or faithful for Christians to go about life speculating on the torments that are deserved by those who sin against them. Nevertheless, it is good for us to know that when men sin against us there will be punishment either now or later, and there will be rewards now or later. When you divide and separate the sheep from the goats, there are eternal consequences. Indeed, John Calvin said in examining this particular article in the Creed that this concern for a moral universe is the real reason why God made it so clear that his Son would come again. The struggle to do what God commands is difficult. Nowhere does the Scripture say that it will be easy. The temptations of life are real. They catch us in their clutches and drag us down. It is hard to live as Christ commands. No one ever promised it would be easy. So, when God has promised through his Son to redeem us, to forgive us, to make us his own, he also promises that he will come again to complete it so that we can have hope in the struggles in which we live.

And finally, there is an eternal, particular destiny prepared for you. Did you notice that the righteous, the sheep, were surprised? Of course they were surprised. Those who know something of the love of God in Jesus Christ have developed a kind of sensitivity about love that would make them surprised. Those who know that God loves them—and how little they deserve it—who know the magnitude of the gift of love in Christ Jesus, become open to the needs of other people. All of the opportunities to love unfold before them. They begin to see how little they accomplish in spite of their best intentions and attempts. Life becomes a matter of trying to see not how little you can get by with, but how much you love. As they do this, their moral sensitivity makes them say, "I do so little. My accomplishments are small."

The Christian preacher in me says that if I get across nothing else, I must say this and get you to hear it: If you have accepted the love of God just barely; if you have responded at all to the salvation in Jesus Christ freely offered and not deserved; if you have tried just a little bit to love as you are loved—then the Second Coming of Jesus Christ is *for* you. There will come that day when you will hear the voice that says, "Come, ye blessed of my Father. Inherit the kingdom prepared for you from the foundation of the world. Inasmuch as you did it unto one of the least of these, my brethren, you did it to me."

Our Lord will come again. Because he will come again, there is meaning and purpose in this life—even if you cannot see it now. Because he will come again, this is a moral universe. Good will be rewarded and evil will be punished, either now or later. Because he will come again, there is an eternal, unique destiny prepared for you.

In the last chapter of the Book of Revelation, the Bible ends with our Lord Jesus saying, "Behold, I am coming soon." The church responds, "Amen. Come, Lord Jesus."

You can live *with* confidence because you can live *on* the promise that "he shall come to judge the quick and the dead."

I *Believe in the Holy Ghost*

John 14:16–17, 25–27

John 16:12–15

"*And I will pray the Father, and he will give you another Counselor, to be with you for ever, even the Spirit of truth, whom the world cannot receive, because it neither sees him nor knows him; you know him, for he dwells with you, and will be in you.*"

John 14:16–17

I Believe in the Holy Ghost

It did not occur to me when I selected the hymn "Open My Eyes That I May See," as it did not occur to me when I was writing the sermon, that this particular hymn conveys not only appropriate words, but also the right mood for talking about the Holy Spirit of God. There is a kind of joyous lilt to this melody. I can remember thinking in the past that something about the Holy Spirit ought to be a great deal more solemn than this. But keep in mind the joy, the bounce, the life, as we talk about the Spirit of God.

I remember some of the first things that our first child did some fifteen or sixteen years ago. It is not that you love the first child more; it is just that when they respond in a particular way, it is the first time for you as parents, and you remember. We would take Beth to a birthday party or perhaps to the park to play. After she got over the shyness, she would run and play with the other children, enjoying the swings, slides, and other playground equipment. She would also run back every now and then and get alongside Mama, or alongside me—to be sure everything was okay. Then she would run back and play. When she fell and hurt herself, if Mama came alongside her quickly and reassuringly, she was usually all right in a moment or two.

The word that Jesus used for the Holy Spirit, the "Comforter" ("Paraclete" is the English transliteration of the Greek), means literally, "the one who is called alongside." That is what Jesus called the Holy Spirit of God. And yet, more frequently, the kinds of attitudes that I sense in people regarding the Holy Spirit are not comfort and joy, but fear, intimidation, or confusion.

If you can think of God as the Father, high and lifted up—way off up yonder, white beard and all, seated on his throne—then you may at least suppose that you can keep him at a distance. He is not at you yet, and even if he comes in a hurry, you will have time to duck; but if God is around you—and even worse, *within* you in the Spirit—then that's scary.

As I was growing up and first pondering the Holy Spirit, I sort of thought of myself as separated from my body—as liquid enough to be poured, and yet light enough to float. I thought about the Spirit of God also as liquid enough to be poured and light enough to float. So, if the Holy Spirit should float into one side of me or be poured into one side of me, probably I would be squeezed out the other. I wasn't sure that I liked the idea of the in-dwelling of the Holy Spirit, or of the Holy Spirit coming upon me. Certainly, I wasn't sure that I wanted the Holy Spirit dwelling within me, because if the Holy Spirit dwelt in there, then I might not have room for me. That's fear.

Also, as I was growing up, I became conscious now and again of people who talked about spiritual things—usually spoken of in a kind of hush or whisper. "Jane is such a spiritual person." "These were things of the Spirit." "Jack is not very spiritual." This was not a part of the Christian jargon of my household, nor of the church I grew up in. You know, we all have jargons—the words and phrases that develop in any group. You have it in your business. Engineers have a jargon. The U.S. Navy has a jargon. The Girl Scouts have a jargon. I have had Girl Scouts in my home, and I know about "sit-upons" and "s'mores" and I know what it means to "fly up." If you don't know about those things, it is because you have never been a Girl Scout or the parent of one. Christians have a jargon, too. We get to talking about what is spiritual and what is not spiritual. I didn't know what that meant. I thought perhaps, "Well, whatever it is, it is not something I am; or, if I am, I don't know about it. So they must be better than I am, or on some kind of higher Christian plane than I am." I felt in-timidated by people who talked about spiritual things.

Lately there has been confusion. It used to be that people who spoke in tongues were Pentecostals and Holy Rollers, and you knew what to think about them. But now there are cultured, well-educated people who are known to be "Charismatic"—as the word goes—who speak in tongues. They feel they have been baptized by the Holy

Spirit in distinction from their previous baptism, and that the Spirit of God tells them certain prophecies that are not available to other people. That's confusing. It has certainly not been the traditional, normal, ordinary style of life of either Protestant or Catholic Christians. Confusion!

It is my task this morning to try to develop, or renew in our minds, a greater sense of the Holy Spirit of God as the Comforter, rather than as the Frightener or the Intimidator, or the Confuser. It is important that we do this because the Holy Spirit is the Third Person of the Trinity—Father, Son, and Holy Spirit; and when we say the Apostles' Creed, this is the third of the three cardinal affirmations:

"I believe in God the Father Almighty . . ."
"I believe in Jesus Christ, His only Son our Lord . . ."
"I believe in the Holy Ghost . . ."

It seems to me the best way of getting at the negative is to speak the positive. What is a spiritual person? That's the personal way of getting at it. How do we experience the Holy Spirit? But before we proceed, I think there are two or three preliminary observations that need to be made.

First of all, let's try to get rid of the spookiness about this. We use in the Creed the archaic words "I believe in the Holy Ghost." We also say, "He shall come to judge the quick and the dead." We know that "quick" means "living," but we don't use it very often. "Ghost," up until recently, meant any spirit—the spirit of a living person or the spirit of a dead person. It did not necessarily mean somebody who has died and is now haunting a house. It meant either the spirit of a human being (living or dead) or God himself who was not confined to a body. It is the person as separate from the body. It is a decent, usable word, but not very familiar. To say "I believe in the Holy Ghost" is simply, purely, equally to say "I believe in the Holy Spirit."

Secondly, and much more importantly, the Holy Spirit is God. The Holy Spirit is not some special agency of God. He is not some special feeling about God. When you encounter the Holy Spirit in any part of life, you are encountering God Almighty. If you were to say, "I was moved by the Spirit," or "led by the Spirit," or "called by the Spirit," it would be just as accurate and would mean exactly the same thing if you would say, "I was moved or led or called by the Lord," or "I was moved or led or called by Jesus Christ," or "I was moved or led or called by God the Father." It is simply more appropriate and more customary when we think of ourselves being acted upon directly and personally by the Lord to speak of him as the Holy Spirit. The Holy Spirit is God. As the Westminster Confession puts it:

> The Spirit of God is God Himself, the Third Person of the Trinity; One God, manifesting Himself in these three Persons. . . . The Holy Spirit, therefore, is to be obeyed, loved, believed in, and worshiped throughout all ages.

Then the third observation in a preliminary way is this: The Holy Spirit should not be a stranger to Presbyterians. If we know our heritage and our theology well, the Spirit of God is more necessary to and ordinary in the fundamentals of believing and living the Christian faith for

Presbyterians than for any Pentecostal or Charismatic I have ever heard of. If you will read the Westminster Confession of Faith asking this question, you will probably be amazed at what you will find. Ask the question, "What does the Holy Spirit do?" and you will hardly find a page in the Westminster Confession of Faith that does not have some answer to that. For, according to Calvinists (those of the Presbyterian or Reformed background), the Holy Spirit convicts us of sin; the Holy Spirit encourages us to repentance; the Holy Spirit moves us to embrace Christ as Savior; the Holy Spirit is the Spirit of adoption that enables us to cry, "Abba, Father"; the Holy Spirit is God as he inspires us to want to serve him; the Holy Spirit is the one who works within us to enable us to obey the Ten Commandments and to try to fulfill the royal law of love. Indeed, the Holy Spirit is the one who inspires Scripture, calls ministers and enables them to proclaim the gospel faithfully and makes for effective teaching and learning. The Holy Spirit is the Spirit of the Church and the Unifier thereof. If one is a hard-and-fast Calvinist, he cannot even conceive of one accepting the fact of his own sin or believing in the Lord Jesus Christ as Savior except as the Holy Spirit inspires him to do so.

But what is a spiritual person like? One who is affected by and inspired by and moved by and in contact with the Holy Spirit of God. A spiritual person is, first of all, a *forgiven person*. That's the first recognizable activity of the Spirit that most of us are aware of. It is the Spirit of God that enables us to face the fact that we are sinners. It is the Spirit of God that enables us finally to understand that Jesus Christ died for us and lives for us. And it is the Holy

Spirit that enables us to move towards him and allow him to turn our lives around.

During the Holy Week services, Mr. Budd, pastor of the First Methodist Church, told the story of an acquaintance of his. She was a young woman who had been wealthy and healthy all her life. She had always gone where she pleased and had done whatever she wanted to do. She had been, in a way, part of the international "jet set." There were no limits of finances or of health. Then, she was struck down with a very painful disease and was hospitalized. This was very difficult for her to face. She had never had to cope with pain before. As the days stretched into weeks and she lay in the hospital bed (which happened to be a bed in a Catholic hospital), she became more and more conscious of a crucifix hanging on the wall—the cross with the figure of Jesus hanging, suffering there. It was opposite where she could not miss it whenever she opened her eyes. She said that at first, as a Protestant, she resented its presence there. Then it started her to thinking of her own position. "Jesus not only died for me, but he suffered in agony for me. He knows even now how I suffer. Indeed, he suffered much greater agony than I have ever suffered. He loves me like that." This was the trigger that set her to confessing her sins, her failures, and her ignoring God. It started turning her around and re-orienting her life towards him. It was the beginning of renewal. Mr. Budd described this lady now as one who lives her life for others.

What brought this about? Well, obviously what brought it about was that God sent his Son to suffer and die for us on that cross. What brought it about is that this young woman knew about that and basically believed it. But what triggered this moment? It could have been a book. It could have been the Bible. It could have been the memory of something that happened to her as a young person. It could have been the words of a minister or a friend or a nurse or just anyone. But God chose that Catholic crucifix hanging on the wall to trigger her confession and repentance and renewal. That's the work of the Holy Spirit. As Jesus said, "The Spirit blows where he will, like the wind." He uses any means that he chooses, but the Spirit is the one who takes the material thing or the words said or the words printed and makes the moment a moment of salvation. The spiritual person is, first of all, a forgiven person, one who is comforted by forgiveness, one for whom the Lord has "come alongside" in grace.

Then, secondly, the spiritual person is a *committed person,* or you might say, an obedient person. The spiritual person is one who does his or her duty. We have just been talking about justification, the process of being saved, and how the Spirit works within us to face up to our sin and accept the salvation freely given in Jesus Christ. Then at the moment of justification, sanctification begins to take place. That means being made holy. It comes from the Latin word *sanctus.* Justification gets you into the presence of God. Sanctification means that you begin to become like him. That also is the work of the Holy Spirit in our lives. The Holy Spirit makes us not only able to begin to obey the Ten Commandments, the Spirit makes us want to. The Spirit makes us not only able in some part to obey the royal law of love—to love the Lord with heart, soul, mind, and strength, and our neighbors as ourselves—but it is the Holy Spirit that constrains us within by the love of Christ to want to.

The Holy Spirit is God's transforming agent; and, therefore, it is the Holy Spirit who grieves when we fail morally or spiritually—and we certainly do that. Yet, the Holy Spirit of God keeps working within us toward the perfection that God requires. So, by the action of the Spirit, we are not only once and for all saved, but we continue the process of being saved. In other words, we are not only justified, but we are becoming sanctified. We not only are forgiven, we are turned around and renewed. The committed person is a spiritual person. Evidence of commitment is at the same time evidence of God's Spirit working quite confidently. An ordinary, Christian-type person who has never had anything very exciting happen spiritually, who obeys Christ with his neighbors, who gives his tithe, who is in the places that he is supposed to be in the church and in the community, who loves his wife and his children and is responsible to them—in general, a person who does his duty—cannot do it except as the Spirit leads him. So, the spiritual person is an obedient person, a person who does his duty, a sanctified person.

Then, thirdly, the spiritual person is an *incorporated person.* I am not talking about incorporated like General Motors and AT&T. I am talking about the basic meaning of the word: "embodiment." Incorporation means to become a part of the body. For the Holy Spirit, you see, is the Spirit of the body—the church. The body is the image that Paul uses most frequently and most predominantly to speak of the church. You can think of all of yourselves as part of one body, members of it, "joined and knit together," as Ephesians says. Maybe I am a fingernail and you are a knuckle and somebody else is a toe, and I hope that we have also some eyes and some hearts in our midst. But with all this variety of gifts and variety of personalities, there is only one Spirit, and that Spirit is the Spirit of the body—the church. The Spirit most predominantly deals with Christians not as individuals, but as fingernails and knuckles and toes and hearts and eyes—parts of the body. "There are many gifts," Paul said, "but only one Spirit." So, those who are spiritual persons are not in the church to be on the roll or there for the record so God will know their name is written in, but they are incorporated people. They are people who are here Sunday after Sunday worshiping. They are people who get involved in learning processes. They are people who pour coffee and who cut the grass and wash windows and teach Sunday School classes and hold committee meetings and support each other and surround each other when there is death or trouble, and call each other on the telephone when somebody is sick, and take a cake by when that is needed. They are involved; they are worshiping; they are participating, living members of the body. The Spirit makes all that happen.

The Spirit of God is our unity. He is what draws us together. He is what enlivens us.

This is the place where you need to say a word or two about the so-called Charismatic movement. It comes from the Greek word *charismata*. It means "gifts—gifts of the Spirit." Always remember that the charismata are gifts for the church. They are for the edification of you—the body. They are for the building up of the body of Christ. Remember that Paul spent that whole beautiful thirteenth chapter of Corinthians talking about using the charismata with love, and they are always to be used with the fruits of the Spirit. You can't have one Spirit in Galatians and another one somewhere else. The fruits of the Spirit are love, joy, peace, long-suffering, et cetera. If someone says, "I have the Spirit of God because I speak in tongues," look closely to see if that gift of tongues (if, indeed, it is a gift) edifies the church. See if it builds up and does not tear down the body of Christ. Look and see if it is displayed with love and with joy and with peace. If, indeed, Charismatics do these things, then they are participating in the Spirit; but simply making noises with tongues or claiming a second baptism does not guarantee the presence of the Spirit of God. If love and the other fruits are absent and if the body is not edified or built up by the "gift of tongues," then we have reason to question their claim of the presence of the Spirit.

The spiritual person is an incorporated person—a living, contributing part of the church.

And then, finally, the spiritual person is a *listening, growing person.* Paul said that "his gifts were that some should be apostles, some prophets, some evangelists, some pastors and teachers, to equip the saints for the work of ministry, for building up the body of Christ." At every point the gifts are for growing and for building. The person who is working with the Spirit is the person who is listening and who is alive. The person who is teaching or preaching is one who has the special possibility that God is working by the power of the Spirit through him or her.

Have you ever been up late on a Saturday night trying

to get a Sunday School lesson ready and it just wouldn't come right? Then you prayed. I have often done that—not by plan, but in desperation—while working on a sermon. "I can't do it. It won't come. There is no way to get the first sentence in there. Help me." The help always comes. That's the work of the Holy Spirit. Anyone who has ever taught young people has felt, "They are not listening to me. They don't ever respond to what I say. I can't get them going in discussion. I don't see that fire in their eyes that they are ready to go out and conquer the world by what I am saying. I am not even sure they have heard a word I have said." Then several years later, a college student catches you at Christmastime and remarks casually that he happens to be living right now by exactly what you taught him in Sunday School. That's the work of the Spirit of God. You find yourself in a circle meeting and the Bible leader is trying her best to get you to think about what Paul wrote in Ephesians. You are thinking about what you have to buy for supper or how you are going to pick up your children, or whatever it is that you are going to do next. You are mentally running down your afternoon list. But she keeps working at you, and finally gets your attention, and you are really inspired by the vision of the immeasurable riches of grace prepared for the saints who sit with the living Christ in glory. A phrase that had never meant anything to you before all of a sudden comes alive for you. You come out of that circle meeting not just feeling better, but changed somehow. The Spirit of God did something in an ordinary circle meeting with a circle Bible leader and a passage of Scripture that the Spirit inspired to be written.

In a moment or two, we will install Peggie Chamblee as our assistant for education. In an earthbound sense, Peggie's job is to find the resources and curricula we need for Church School and other programs. It is her job to provide for the training of teachers. It is her job to be counselor, friend, helper, and encourager of all the people involved with youth work and with the church school. Her job involves an enormous load of details. Everybody always wants Peggie to get something for them, find something for them, or tell them what they ought to use. In one way you can say, "Now this is just simply an administrative job where you keep up with a lot of details." You could also say, "This is a way in which an open path is cleared away for the Holy Spirit to work in our learning and growth." If you say that, you can say that her task is profoundly spiritual in nature, for the spiritual person is a listening, growing person.

The Holy Spirit of God is alive and at work. If you are forgiven, you know him in your forgiveness. If you are committed, you know him as the power that presses you to obey. If you are incorporated into the church, the Spirit puts you there. If you are growing, you are experiencing the work of the Spirit in growth.

Do not be afraid or confused, and let no one confuse you. Rather, rejoice and be glad and feel confident. God who loved you enough to die for you is at work within and around you. He cannot be defeated, and neither can you.

The Holy Catholic Church

Exodus 19:1–8

Matthew 16:13–20

"I will give you the keys of the kingdom of heaven, and whatever you bind on earth shall be bound in heaven, and whatever you loose on earth shall be loosed in heaven."

—Matthew 16:19

The Holy Catholic Church

The other day as I was with a fellow minister, I walked behind a van in a parking lot. Above the bumper was a little sign. On it were the words "Polar Bear" and a number. I wondered out loud what that meant. "That's his 'handle,'" I was told. Of course. He operates a citizen's band radio in his van. Six months or a year ago, I would have recognized a man's "handle," but now the fad is passing, and people like me who do not have C.B.'s just are not thinking about them anymore. The fickle crowd is out looking for other fads to enhance the meaning of life.

There was a time after World War II and in the fifties, when going to church was a fad. It was what everybody did. It was, indeed, for many a useful social organization in the community. Then the fad passed. Now it seems to be shifting again. It seems to me that there are more people asking questions and more coming to church for answers. There are more college students in church services (and other ministers confirm this) than there were a few years ago. Some young couples become a part of the church even before their children are of Sunday School age. You didn't see that often a few years ago. It seems to me that in a strange sort of way this puts the church in a position of crisis—not the kind of crisis that says, "We are desperate. What will we do?" but the kind of crisis that says, "Things are going well. What shall we do?"

We could, of course, say to ourselves, "Well, let's just ride the wave and enjoy our good fortune" (or the blessing of God, whichever way you want to put it), or we could say, "Let's be sure that the deeper questions that are being asked get answered. Let's be sure that we enable the people who come to church to really be the church and not just fool around on the surface of the church."

Where do we get guidelines for the church in this kind of crisis? It appears that Jesus himself faced a similar crisis in his ministry at about the time he took his disciples on a retreat to the foothills of Mount Hermon, to the springs that are the headwaters of the River Jordan. They called the place Caesarea Philippi. It was a sparsely populated area of natural beauty, a place to draw aside and think. There Jesus asked his disciples, "Who do men say that I am?" Then, "Who do you say that I am?" There was reason for asking this. There had developed—if you will permit the word—a kind of fad to follow Jesus. He was an unusual speaker and teacher. He spoke with an authority unlike the scribes and Pharisees. He healed people. He had no hesitation to challenge some of the comfortable practices of the scribes and Pharisees. But then things changed. The opposition to Jesus became serious. It became risky and somewhat dangerous to be identified with him. And besides that, what Jesus was doing was familiar. He had passed the crest of popular enchantment.

John remarked that at about this time many who had followed after Jesus turned away from him. Jesus turned to his disciples and asked, "Will you also go away?" It was here that Peter responded, "To whom shall we go? You have the words of eternal life." At Caesarea Philippi, when Jesus asked, "Who do you say that I am?" Peter put it more succinctly as he replied, "You are the Christ, the Son of the living God." Do you sense the excitement and enthusiasm of Jesus' response? "Blessed are you, Simon, son of John. Flesh and blood did not reveal this to you, but my Father in heaven." In other words, "You've got it! You understand!"

When you face your own crisis, you ask about the church of Jesus Christ as Peter did about Jesus himself, "Am I simply following a fad, or am I into something with more depth?" Then you try to see what the church really is. Your own observations surprise you. You come up with something not created by flesh and blood, something that is different, something that is distinct, something that is unique, something that is unprecedented, something that is unparalleled, something holy. You see, that's what the word "holy" means. It does not mean pure or perfect. It means distinct and different—as God is distinct and different. Jesus was saying, as he talked about founding his church, that flesh and blood did not reveal it.

Look at any other organization or grouping of people. They are pulled together from the creative imaginations of human beings of flesh and blood, out of the motivations of human beings of flesh and blood, or through the organizational skills of human beings of flesh and blood, by the persuasive powers of individuals or human beings of flesh and blood, and for the purposes of human beings of flesh and blood. No other institution on earth except the church was initiated by God the Father, given command and identity and possibility of response by God the Son, and actually called out by God the Holy Spirit.

The Greek word for "church" is *ecclesia,* which means "those who are called out," or "called together." By whom? By the Holy Spirit of God. One here and another there and someone somewhere else and somebody over there looks upon Jesus dying on the cross and living again, and the Spirit enables them to respond. The Spirit calls us out to be separate, calls us to be distinct, calls us to be the church. That's what it means when we say that the church is holy. It is absolutely different, absolutely unique, absolutely unprecedented, absolutely unparalleled. It will not be duplicated. We are holy because we are different. That is a part of what we must communicate to a world that comes asking questions.

We are also catholic. Jesus said to Peter, "You are the rock." The Greek word *petros* means "rock." "Upon this rock I will found my church." But it is catholic—not in the sense in which our Roman Catholic friends have traditionally understood it. The Roman Catholic Church has for generations believed that Jesus appointed Peter as a person, as a human being, to go and found and govern the church. Consequently, the Catholic popes as the Bishops of Rome all down through the centuries have seen themselves as the legitimate successors to Peter. As persons, they ruled the church. I find very little evidence anywhere else in the New Testament that this is what Jesus meant. It appears from the Book of Acts that James (the brother of Jesus) and Paul had at least as much authority in the early church as Peter did. It appears also that the Holy Spirit—not Peter—was authorized to govern the church. But then what *did* Jesus mean? Was the "rock" Peter's character or, perhaps, his strength of commitment? Not long after, Jesus said that this same Peter would deny him three times. It was hardly Peter's character that was the foundation of the church, any more than it is your character or mine. None of us are good enough for that, are we? We couldn't expect that even of Peter.

Well, what about Peter's words of commitment: "You are the Christ, the Son of the living God"? They are great words, necessary words, living words. Yet, you and I can say words, too. There are all those who become members of this church who promise that they will serve Christ with us with their time and their talents and their means as God gives them opportunity; but frankly, there are more opportunities than I see performances. Every young person or any other who comes by profession of faith promises that they will serve Christ by supporting and participating in the worship and work of this congregation to the *best* of their ability. Most of us live by less than our words, don't we? It was not the words of Peter upon which Jesus Christ founded his church.

The only understanding that makes any sense to me is to say that the rock is the response of faith. Faith can grow strong and weak. It can rise and it can diminish. It can sometimes be more clearly displayed and sometimes less clearly displayed. But faith remains. Paul said, "By grace are you saved through faith." It is Peter's response to Jesus Christ—not faith out of a vacuum, but response to a living Lord who would die for him and who would live for him, and whom Peter knew face-to-face. It is that response that makes the church catholic, or universal, or ecumenical. Use whichever word feels most comfortable to you.

In this very key, fundamental, essential way we are identical with all Christians, not only geographically, but chronologically—those who are far and those who are near, those who have come before and those who will come after. In a very fundamental way, we are identical with the Christians of the first century. We are identical with those who were persecuted in the Roman arena. We are identical with the Crusaders. We are identical with the pious monks and nuns of the Middle Ages. We are identical with the Christians of the Reformation in Geneva, Edinburgh, Wittenberg, Strasbourg, Paris, and all those other places. We are identical with the Christians of colonial New England and the revivals of the nineteenth century on the frontier and with the social gospel movement at the turn of the century. Because wherever all of us, or any of us, respond at the core of our being in faith to Jesus Christ, we are then a part of the Holy Catholic, or Holy Universal, or Holy Ecumenical Church. We have our differences. We are not identical in all ways. All those other folks who don't do it like Presbyterians are wrong in some respects—or so we like to think—but they and we are the church. It is not the quality or the perfection of our ideas or practices that establishes our identity as the church; it is our response in faith to the Lord Jesus Christ.

So, the church is holy and the church is catholic, and part of what we need to display and need to be for a questioning world is a church that recognizes all of us, and somehow enables us to work together—all of us—for the building of the kingdom.

And then, the church is you and me—with all our flaws, with all our weaknesses, with all our mistakes, with all our blemishes, with all our blind spots. The church is not the building or the organization. The church is you and me and our brothers and sisters everywhere—the Holy Catholic Church.

How can we be sure? How can we trust ourselves? How can we know that we are doing the things by which the world can identify a body that is unique and profound and can answer the deep questions of life? What are the foundations on which we can stand in order to live? What are the purposes toward which we should aim that are of worth? And what kind of hopes can we have for this Holy Catholic Church? We can go on to answer those questions by looking at the rest of Jesus' response to Peter: "You are Peter, and upon this rock I will found *my* church." Notice the pronoun: *my* church. It is always the Lord's church. It is useful sometimes to say, "Oh, that's Mr. Speed's church over there," but it isn't my church. It belongs to Jesus Christ. It makes me uncomfortable when any of us talk about "our church." It doesn't belong to us. It is useful, practical identification, and sometimes it is okay to use the term in order to explain that we are talking about "our church" and not "their church" as long as we are aware that it belongs to none of us. It belongs to him. He is the head of it. He should be the center of its activity and the focus of its worship. It is good for us to eat together. It is good for us to have recreation together. It is good for us to study together. It is good for us to engage in wholesome community activities together. It is good for us to plan and build buildings. But at the point when a stranger comes in, very quickly we need to show that stranger that at the center of all this is Jesus Christ. If we let him get out on the periphery of our things and of our activities, then we have allowed ourselves to get out on the periphery of the Holy Catholic Church. "Upon this rock I will found *my* church." Our Book of Church Order still says that Jesus Christ is the Head of the church.

"And the gates of hell shall not prevail against it," he said. An ancient city was protected by a great wall, but the strongest and largest parts of the fortification were the gates, for the gates were not just wooden things to swing back and forth and let people in and out. The gates had to be big towers with armories and rooms from which armed men could sally forth to attack the attackers. The sally port was always a part of the gate structure. It was the source of counterattack. To say that the gates of hell shall not prevail against the church is to say that the strongest, most powerful fortifications that Satan or his legions can command cannot defeat the church.

That's not all. The clear implication here is that the

powers of evil are in a defensive position. They are inside the fortification. They are fighting off an invader. Who is that invader? It is the church—the church roaming and marching freely outside the walls, on the offensive against evil. One day the evil will be defeated. The church is not on the defensive—not at its best. The church is on the offensive. Its task is always to conquer evil where it finds it—in an individual person through evangelism, in society through social action. The church is the mighty army of God reaching out in love and compassion to defeat evil in a person or in a community. You can tell if it is really the church by whether it is on the offensive or not.

And then, finally, Jesus promised, "I will give you the keys to the kingdom of heaven." He did not say, "I will give you the kingdom." He did not say, "I am going to lay it all out there for you perfectly." He said, "I am going to give you a struggle that you will win." A key in Jesus' time was probably a two-handed affair. You had to put it through a heavy oaken door and work it with both hands in order to turn the big latch. Sure, we are not perfect. We have our shortcomings, our failures, our shortsightedness. We don't even look like the church sometimes when we are fussing at our children or when we forget to do our homework or when we are honking the horn at some idiot who turns in front of us on the freeway. We were never promised that it would be easy, but we are given a struggle that we can win—we have the keys. So, wherever you find the church as it should be, you find confidence and hope.

Jesus said that it is his church, and you will find him in the middle of it. Jesus said that the gates of hell shall not prevail against it, and so you will find the church on the offensive. Jesus said, "I will give you the keys of the king-dom . . . ," and you will find the church in a struggle which it will win—a church having hope.

When I was first out of seminary, I was asked to go to see a widower with several children who did not come to church. He was known to be something of a skeptic and an agnostic. I was a little frightened, and I put it off as long as I could. Finally, I went to his home. The doorway of his Spanish-type ranch house was recessed. It was dark and forbidding, I thought. As I rang the doorbell, I could see no lights. I sincerely hoped that no one would be at home. Shortly, a face appeared at the door. It was not a hostile face, but it was not a hospitable face, either. I think all I got was, "Yes?" I had to explain my mission and identify myself and I finally stated that several people had asked me to come. There was no enthusiasm about it, but he did step back and open the door. I walked into a sparsely fur-nished home. The furniture that was there was of a Span-ish style. The living room into which I was escorted was cold and dark. There was no carpet on the floor. The room desperately needed light and a woman's touch. He seated me in a straight, hard armchair. He then proceeded to walk fifteen or twenty feet across the room and seat himself in a straight, hard armchair. His arrangements were not cal-culated for long conversations. Then he waited. I tried to tell him about the church of Jesus Christ, and why he needed to bring his children, and what it could mean to him. I thought of every reason at my command, of what the Scripture says and of what I had experienced. I even tried to cite a couple of well-known theologians whose names he might know. There was silence. Finally, he said,

"The church is a useful social institution in a community, and I guess yours is as good as any." Still, I took what I could get. I invited him to start coming to church and to bring his children. If he came only believing he was touching something good for the community, while he was there he might discover the Lord who made it good—and so much more.

His words have stayed with me a long, long time. Perhaps there was a hardness of heart there that made him see the church in that way, but perhaps he was seeing what the church sometimes shows itself to be—a useful social institution in a community. We can do better than that.

For the church is holy. It is absolutely unique, unprecedented, unparalleled, distinct from all other bodies and organizations. The church is catholic wherever we find it. Jesus Christ is the fundamental core. The gates of hell shall not prevail against it. It always has the keys to the kingdom. The church is you and me—weak, blemished, incomplete, imperfect, impure. We need to admonish each other and correct each other and try to change each other; but most of all, we need to rejoice, be glad, be thankful, and get about the glorious business of being the Holy Catholic Church.

The Communion of Saints

Deuteronomy 6:10–13

I Corinthians 1:4–9

God is faithful, by whom you
were called into the fellowship of his
Son, Jesus Christ our Lord.
—I Corinthians 1:9

The Communion
of Saints

We are human beings. It is our nature to need each other. The desire to be a part of the life of others varies in intensity from time to time, but it never disappears.

When I was a small boy, milk was served, not in cardboard cartons, but in little half-pint bottles. The bottles were sealed with tops that were circular disks with handles that you could lift with your fingernail. In the first grade I organized a bottle top club. We joined forces to collect milk bottle tops. There was a need to be together.

After World War I, the German people were defeated, disillusioned. Many of the old ties were broken. Because of people's need to be a part of something and a part of each other, millions of Germans were drawn into the Hitler Youth, the Brown Shirts, the S.S. Troops and various other Nazi organizations which were built on prejudice, hatred, and a sense of national superiority. Nevertheless, the need for identification was so great that they overlooked the evils.

A young man and a young woman, following Scripture and the inner urgency in themselves, will leave their parents and cleave unto each other. The two shall become one because they need intimacy. They need to be one with somebody. They need to belong. Paul says that this intimacy of marriage is symbolic of Christ and his church.

When someone dies, the one who is widowed must find new relationships and adjust old relationships. It may take a long time. It may be very painful, but it is absolutely necessary in order to continue to live. We need each other.

So, in the Apostles' Creed—in association with the affirmation about the Holy Spirit and as a part of our affirmation about the Holy Catholic Church—we say we believe in the communion of saints. We are not just pointing out there into the future towards the ideal for a Christian church, but we are also affirming a unique and present relationship that God has provided for us and given to us. Everywhere the church really exists, there is the communion now.

Let me use as my illustration the church in Corinth in the first century A.D. If there could be a communion of the saints in Corinth, it could be anywhere. Corinth was a commercial center. It contained a mixed population of Greeks and Romans and just about everybody else. It had all the good and the evil you could expect in a bustling port city. We have only to read Paul's letters, particularly the first letter, to perceive that the Christian community itself had the problems you might expect in such a city. There was open dissension. Some said, "I follow Paul," and some said, "I belong to Peter." Others said, "Apollo is my leader," and, I am sure with an air of superiority, there were those who said, "I belong to Christ."

They didn't know what to do with women in that church. They had a women's liberation movement, and they weren't sure about what role women should play.

They didn't know whether they were supposed to eat meat that was offered to idols. There was immorality—open immorality—and even sexual perversion, and the leaders in the church hadn't done anything to stop it or to put the guilty parties out of the church.

Some of them were so greedy and so callous that they came to the Lord's Table, bringing abundant provisions to stuff themselves and to get drunk while others went without.

Their theological problems were so deep that some were not even sure they believed that Jesus had risen from the dead or that they themselves could rise from the dead in faith.

And if all this were not enough, there was a charismatic movement in the church. They were in an uproar over those who were speaking in tongues. And yet, Paul begins his letter by affirming that they have been called into fellowship with Jesus Christ, into the communion of the saints; they have been enriched in him with everything that they need in spiritual gifts; and on the foundation of the fellowship or communion of the saints, they can solve their problems.

Now, I think that is more than remarkable. I think that means if Corinth had a communion of the saints, then we certainly do. We may have our problems, but we are not as bad off as they were.

I doubt that there is anyone here who has grown so satisfied with his or her own relationship with the Lord's church but what he or she hungers for relationships that are deeper, broader, and more meaningful. I guess that every one of us from time to time asks, "What's wrong with me? What have I done wrong? Why am I not closer to more people than I am?" I don't think the answer here is to say, "How can I go out and get the communion of the saints?" but rather, the answer is first to say, "What is it? Where does it come from? How can I get it? How can I strengthen it among us, and particularly for myself?"

The word *communion* is in the Greek *koinonia*. Some of you are familiar with it because it was printed in large letters across the brochure that we used with our Phase I campaign. *Koinonia* is sometimes translated "communion," sometimes "fellowship," sometimes "partnership," sometimes "participation," sometimes "taking part," and sometimes simply "sharing." It is a very prominent and important word in the New Testament. It is a key word in understanding what the life of the church was about in the first century A.D. It is probably easier to point to the circumstances of *koinonia,* or communion, or fellowship than it is to describe exactly what these relationships were like. Perhaps the most helpful thing I can do is to point to certain situations where the word *koinonia* was used indicating that the "communion of saints" was being experienced, and then try to give you a feel of what that communion was like and is like today.

In this passage I just read in Paul's first Letter to the Corinthians, the word appears as "fellowship." "You were called into the fellowship of his Son Jesus Christ . . ." (or the communion of his Son, and thus with each other). Then having identified the relationship among them as communion of the saints, Paul moves from that base to call for an end to all the disagreements and dissensions among them.

In the letter to the Philippians he writes, "If there is any encouragement in Christ, if there is any incentive of love, if there is any participation (*koinonia,* communion, fellowship) in the Spirit, then complete my joy by being of one mind." Probably the most prominent thrust of the idea of the communion of the saints is unity, or the movement toward unity. There is always something of that unity about us, and it is because the Spirit of God is working in us. When we are truly Christian, when we are truly a part of the church, we move together and not apart. To be sure, there have been times in history (and we have observed one recently) where parts of the church will separate from other parts, maybe for good reasons, but no one really feels comfortable about it. Somehow or other, we cannot approach the cross in separate lines, not speaking to each other, as we make confession of sins and stand to receive forgiveness. Where there is the communion of saints gathered around our Lord, there is a kind of compelling force that pulls us toward each other as we are pulled towards him.

I can give you a long list of problems in the ecumenical movement. I can give you a list of why there would be difficulty in uniting with our closest brothers and sisters in the Northern or United Presbyterian Church. And yet, something in me that is scriptural and of the Spirit says that some day, some way, we must come closer together rather than being drawn further apart. The Spirit of Christ is the Spirit of unity. The communion of the saints is characterized—within this congregation, among congregations, within a denomination, among denominations—by a compelling force towards, not division, but unity.

Another place where this word *koinonia* is used is in the second chapter of the Book of Acts. Peter had preached and several thousand people had believed, made confession of sin and given profession of faith. They were all together: attending to the apostles' teaching, to fellowship (*koinonia*), the breaking of bread, and to prayers. Let me tell you something. No matter how good you are, how gentle you are, how understanding you are, how vigorous you are, how creative you are, how energetic you are, or what beautiful organizations you can make in this church, what we have together on the horizontal plane is totally dependent upon what we have together on the vertical plane. Our fellowship is dependent upon our relationship to God through Jesus Christ, unequivocally. You will always find the communion of the saints in the context of the preaching of the Word. What we are doing here is the center of the church's life, because where the gospel is preached and the Word of God is expounded is where we are reminded of the Almighty, where we reach upward to God in worship, and where we listen to hear his Word proclaimed, and to be pulled together and made alive. You will always find the communion of saints in its most visible reality where the saints have gathered attending to the apostles' teaching.

And there is a place in the beginning of the Letter to the Philippians where Paul gives thanks to God for their partnership with him in the Gospel. Here *koinonia* is translated "partnership." There is always about the communion of the saints a devotion to the causes of God that are larger than our own particular human personal causes. In his Second Letter Paul invites the church at Corinth to take part in the offering for the helping of the saints in Judaea. Taking part is *koinonia,* again the same word. And there is the sense in which we are most the church, most in communion with each other—when we join together for the glory of God, for causes that are bigger than things that you and I could even imagine, bigger even than the physical necessities of life. We touched on it when we joined together in committing part of our resources to build Holland Hall.

But that was just touching on it. Some years ago I was privileged as a college student to work in Montreat during those weeks when the missionaries who were going out for the first time were brought together for their final training and commissioning. I sensed a communion of the saints there that I could not be a part of, at least at that time. It was not because they wished to exclude me. Indeed, they tried to include everybody they could. But what they had was the realization that every one of them had committed themselves to proclaim the gospel of Jesus Christ in some other country, regardless of the cost. There are others who have made equal commitments, but these were open and shared. You could sense the spiritual electricity among those people. Al Harris can tell you today how he feels about the other missionary families who were in Montreat with him and Gerrie that summer when they were trained, commissioned, and sent out.

Several years later, as a staff member of one of our boards, I also had the privilege of being in Blue Ridge across the valley from Montreat in that summer when several hundred of our missionaries in the Belgian Congo (now Zaïre) were refugees. Independence had exploded into revolution. Some of our missionaries got out with the clothes on their backs. I sat in the back as Dr. Darby Fulton tried to talk with the missionaries and they to him about this experience. There was not terror or fear, only shock; and in that shock, a mighty affirmation of the glory of God, of what he had done with them and would do in the Congo.

There is about the communion of the saints a sense of partnership with God and loyalty to God in causes of his that are greater than ours. You can't really get the communion of saints fully without a commitment to more than your own selfish interests, without a commitment to partnership in God's causes.

And then, in the communion of saints there is a deep respect and caring about the others who also are part of that communion, or fellowship, those who are along with you. Strangely, the word shows up with Paul in discussing meat offered to idols, of all things. He talks about what they should do because they participate in the body of Christ, the church. Now you and I know, and they knew, that idols are not anything. An idol is a piece of wood or a piece of metal or a piece of stone or a piece of clay. Just because some pagan people have carried a side of beef into the temple and laid it on an altar and said that it was dedicated to Zeus or Apollo or Diana doesn't make it so. Zeus and Apollo and Diana don't exist, for heaven's sake. So, a Christian was perfectly free, if the meat was good, to eat it and ask no questions—*except* when there was a new Christian with a weak conscience. When you are with someone who had before worshiped idols and dedicated meat to idols, and who is so new and so weak that he could be tempted to fall back into dependence upon idols, and because of his conscience feels that he must refuse the meat offered to idols, then you also restrain yourself.

Must not the same thing be said today among the communion of saints? You and I may be free to do a great number of things, but if there is someone present whose conscience may be hurt, we must restrain ourselves for the weaker brother or sister. Is it not also true that you and I are constrained to do certain things, not because you and I need them in the life of the church, but because weaker brothers and sisters need them? Wouldn't it help all the weaker brothers and sisters if everyone here made just the simple commitment to be in worship every Sunday morning, if not for your own sake, for the sake of the weaker brother or sister who needs your support? The communion of saints is always about respect for the others in caring, or to put it another way, for loving each other as Jesus loved us.

Unity, attending to the Word, partnership in God's causes, respect in caring for each other, and finally, sharing in the suffering of our Lord. Now that's a strange one, isn't it? But those are the words that Paul uses: "*Koinonia* in his suffering." It is easy for us to accept the idea that we are to follow Christ in moral purity, in love for neighbors, in doing good deeds, in teaching what he taught and living as he wants us to live. It may not be so easy for us to swallow that we are to follow him in his suffering.

Probably most of us here will never be called upon to be physically tortured, to give up freedom or children or home or anything else of great value for the Lord's sake. It may be that we will never have cause to fear for our lives because of Christian commitment. But there are many of you here who have been passed over for promotion because you refused to cut corners and to carry on unethical practices in business. There are some of you who have lost the opportunity to make a great deal of money because you would not pass money under the table. When you and I suffer for what we believe by exclusion or by being cheated or being set apart, we need to share that suffering with one another so that by being supported by others who have suffered in like manner, we can love those who have harmed us rather than being embittered and angered. We who have not suffered need to be open to sharing the suffering of others who are hurt or excluded because they stand for the Lord Jesus Christ in a secular world.

Can you get more of the feel of it? Do you identify the places where you experience the communion of the saints as you are literally drawn toward unity and feel uncomfortable when you try to pull apart—as you attend to the preaching of the Word, as you join together in God's causes bigger than your own, as you love one another as Christ loved you, as you share suffering together?

How do you get such communion of the saints? Where does it come from? It is a gift. You don't get it. You don't earn it. You accept it. Remember the words of Moses talking about the life those people would live across the river in the Promised Land, a sort of precursor of the life of the Christian church. "Look over there," Moses said. "There are cities you did not build; there are houses filled with good things you did not fill; there are cisterns hewed out for the water that you did not hew; there are vineyards and olive trees planted there that you did not plant." Did you create the fellowship of the saints you now know? Did you make it happen? No. It goes back beyond your father and mother and your grandparents and your great-grandparents. You did not even build the building we worship in, nor did I. Where did it all start? Doesn't it start in the heart of God who chose in his grace to decide to forgive you and redeem you? Didn't it continue in the willingness of the Lord Jesus Christ to lay down his life for you? Didn't it proceed in the whole procession of apostles and prophets and saints all through the centuries? You and I are made saintly, made holy, made righteous—not by our own deserving, but by God's gift in Jesus Christ. It continues to be a gift as others pass it on.

How did you get here, or to the first church of your life? I don't know about you, but my mother and daddy took me by the hand and took me to a Sunday School class. I guess I sat in my daddy's lap in church until I was old enough to sit by myself. I had my hands slapped sometimes when I misbehaved. I got encouragement when I got discouraged. There are many of you who have fallen away and who have come back. Who brought you back? Who invited you? Who made you a part of their life so they could make you a part of the church? The communion of the saints! We did not deserve it; we did not earn it; we have not gotten it for ourselves. It is one of the most precious gifts our Lord Jesus left on earth for us.

What do you do with a gift? Well, the answer is obvious. What do you do with a Christmas gift or a birthday gift? What does the giver want you to do with a gift? Enjoy it. Enjoy it. Let yourself go with the force that pulls us together in greater unity. Let that urge that says, "Be in the place where the Word is preached and God is worshiped," be acknowledged—give in to that urge frequently, regularly, whenever it comes. Just let go: give in to it. Find yourself at least one cause that God really cares about in which you have no selfish interest whatsoever. Let go into some cause that is bigger than any human being or any human devising. Let yourself go. Let that instinct to love your neighbors have its way, so that you love even the narrow ones, even the ones you disagree with. Let that instinct have full play in your life. And let yourself be open to those who suffer, and share your sufferings for Christ's sake with others.

Bottle cap clubs, country clubs, political clubs, hobby clubs, retired persons clubs, tennis clubs. I am told that there is even a procrastinators' club! We need each other. We need to be a part of others, to share ourselves. The biblical way, the best way, the way which by nature we were created, the way most fulfilling for us—is the communion of the saints.

The Forgiveness of Sins

Psalm 32

Acts 5:27–32

Blessed is he whose transgression is forgiven, whose sin is covered.
—*Psalm 32:1*

The Forgiveness
of Sins

A week or so ago, an experienced mountain climber took a day off from his job and scaled the world's tallest building from the outside. Briefly, he captured the attention of a large part of New York City and much of the world. We are always interested in a cause for which someone will risk his life. We may not believe in that cause or adopt it for ourselves, but when someone risks his life it does arouse our curiosity. When someone really important whom we deeply respect risks his life for a cause, then we ask ourselves a different set of questions: Does this make demands upon me? Should I risk what he risked? Should I offer what he offered? Should I commit myself at the level he has committed himself?

Such a man was Simon Peter, and such a cause was creating a furor in Jerusalem in the very earliest days of the Christian church. The chief priests, the Sadducees, felt themselves threatened and finally took the leaders of the cause and threw them into prison. At that moment, literally all of the Christians were in Jerusalem, or very close by. It was probably thought, "If we stamp it out now, we will stamp it out forever." When the bars closed behind Peter and the others, they inevitably asked questions. You and I know that Peter had a long life ahead of him and that he would have worse threats than this, but Peter had no way of knowing that. For all he knew, this was the last night of his life.

I have never been a prisoner, but I have visited in jails; I have preached in jails; I spent a summer working in a mental hospital where in every ward the doors are locked behind you. Even when you know you can get out (or at least you believe you can), it is a strange feeling to hear the clank of the lock behind you. I can imagine the feeling one must have when you know that the sound of the bolt being driven home means that you are the one who is being locked in and they intend to keep you there. When that happens, you ask questions about what you did. Was it worth it? Was the cost too high? If I ever get out of here, would I do it again?

That very night the angel came; and, by some mysterious way known only to God, Peter and the others were led out without disturbing either the gates or the guards. Do you know what they did? They went right back to what they had been doing before. The Scripture tells us that at daybreak they were teaching in the temple again.

That's what they had been arrested for! They didn't even go home to change clothes and eat breakfast or to pause and then think about it. Why? What cause is worth the risk of imprisonment? What cause is worth the risk of death?

They were preaching about something they called "that life" or "that way." They were preaching about Jesus who had been crucified and then raised from the dead. They were teaching about something that he did. He gave repentance to Israel; he gave a turning around, a change of mind or a change of heart, the possibility of a new life; and then the forgiveness of sins. That, my friends, is, as they say, "the bottom line." That's what it is all about: the forgiveness of sins.

Christmas is about the forgiveness of sins. That's why Jesus was born in Bethlehem. Jesus teaching on the mountain, Jesus healing along the shore, Jesus standing out in the boat preaching—that's about the forgiveness of sins. The way of life he lived is about the forgiveness of sins. His death on the cross is specifically because of sin and for the forgiveness of sins. The resurrection is about triumph in the forgiveness of sins. The forgiveness of sins was what all the furor in Jerusalem was about.

Of course, the chief priests were threatened. God forgives sins; and if he forgives through this Jesus, then why do you need priests or sacrifices at the altar? The forgiveness of sins is why Peter was willing to risk his life again and again and again; and so would Paul, and so would James, and so would Thomas, and so would all the others. That's the central point. This, for us—for you and me personally—is what the Apostles' Creed is all about. It is, of course, important and wonderful that God is like thus-

and-so, that Jesus Christ is like thus-and-so, and that the Holy Spirit is like thus-and-so. But if we do not come down to the point where we can say, "God has had mercy upon me, my sins are forgiven and my life is made new," then it really does not have anything to do with you and me. The forgiveness of sins is the point towards which that whole grand and awful procession of events that God was carrying out in Jesus Christ moves. It is from that point that life can become new and you and I can move into the future.

Before we accept the forgiveness of our sins, you and I are as men and women paralyzed, unable to live fully. After we understand that our sins are forgiven, there is nothing in the world that can contain us. For, you see, sin is the problem. It is *the* problem. It has always been *the* problem. We may define the problem as a political problem or an engineering problem or a chemical problem; but, basically, all of the things we have to solve are human problems, and human problems have as their root: sin. These problems are complicated by sin.

The manager of a Penney's Store once told me, "Jim, as we say down on the floor where everything is bought and sold, it is not really the problem that disturbs us—it's the politics of the problem." It's the people. And people sin. If you can get at sin, you can get at anything that troubles us.

The Shorter Catechism says, "Sin is any want of conformity unto, or transgression of, the law of God."

Sin involves both what we do and what we fail to do; or, as an old and wonderful prayer that you know well states it, "We have left undone those things which we ought to have done; and we have done those things which we ought not to have done; and there is no health in us." That's sin.

Those who have spent their lives studying the Bible tell us that, basically, the Bible talks about sin in three ways. It speaks of sin as *rebellion against God*, as *alienation or estrangement from God*, and as *missing the mark*.

Jesus' parable of the Prodigal Son illustrates all three and shows their interrelatedness to each other. The son decided that he knew better than the father. Isn't that where sin begins? We know better than God. "You know, God, you may like it that way, but I really know better. Give me my inheritance now." So, he takes it and goes into a far country. That's rebellion. That's disobedience. It says, "I know better than God." He goes into a far country and wastes it on riotous living. He tries to put as many miles between himself and God as he can. Of course, you can't really do that in a physical sense, because God is everywhere. But in a spiritual and emotional sense you can estrange yourself from God, both by going to places you know God doesn't want you to go and by doing things you know God doesn't want you to do—whether those things are riotous or not. That's estrangement, or alienation. To the best the Prodigal Son could do it, he alienated himself from the father—from God, in Jesus' understanding. Then when the famine came, he had used it all up. He found himself trying to survive by feeding somebody's pigs. He was precisely 180 degrees around from his own God-given potential. He had missed the mark. In trying to find his life by doing it his own way, he had fouled his life up. He was disobedient, alienated, and off-target!

Do I need to illustrate further by talking about wasted lives; by talking about public scandal; by talking about fouled-up marriages; by talking about the horrors of war; by talking about all of the cruelties that we perpetrate on one another by word and deed, by commission and omission? Don't they all involve in one way or another our saying, "I know better than you do, God. I am going to do it my way. I am going to put as much distance between myself and you, God, as I can"? Then we say, "Lord, why is it I missed the mark? Why did I mess it all up? I don't understand." That's the problem. That's sin.

The answer to sin is forgiveness. Let's be very clear about that. Some would say, "Oh, if you could just teach everybody and show them the difference between right and wrong, they would all be all right." Every good religion in the world has done that for centuries. But good teaching doesn't make people good. The secular philosophers can tell you the difference between right and wrong. But how do you get people to do the right and keep from doing the wrong?

Once when I was a little boy, I saw my mother put a little jar of chocolate chips up in the cabinet. As she left the kitchen she said, "Don't eat those." And I did. How do you keep little boys from eating chocolate chips when nobody is watching?

Thomas Carlyle, the great British historian from the last century, who had at least pondered the answers to mankind's problems, once took his mother to church. Riding home in the buggy, his mother asked his opinion of the sermon. In some exasperation he said, "If I were the preacher, I would simply stand in the pulpit and say, 'You people know what you ought to do. Go and do it.'" His mother let a decent amount of time pass, and then she replied quietly, "Aye, Thomas. And would you tell them how?"

The solution to sin is not simply teaching what's right and wrong. Jesus was superb in that. But that was not Jesus' point. Jesus' point was forgiveness.

"While we were yet sinners, Christ died for us." That was what God intended. That was what he was about in Jesus Christ—to work, to reveal, to display, to make effective forgiveness.

"For God so loved the world that he gave his only Son, that whoever believes in him should not perish but have everlasting life." And Paul caught that sense of grace. "By grace are you saved through faith; not by works, lest any man should boast."

Let me tell you something. It's free. It is given. It is not earned. There are no ifs, there are no conditions, there are no prerequisites. You don't have to be any special kind of person. You don't have to be good. You don't have to have a good name. You don't have to stand high in the community. You don't have to have great accomplishments, or little accomplishments. You don't have to be pretty. You don't have to be handsome. You don't have to be in the right crowd. You don't have to be associated with the right church. God forgives you as you are.

Some would say, "Yes, but Jesus had to die. It was a kind of bargain. God's not really merciful. Jesus bought him off." Oh, yes, Jesus is the propitiation for our sins. He did satisfy God's sense of justice and perfection. But long before Jesus died, long before Jesus taught, long before he was born in Bethlehem, it was God's intention to forgive. Never forget that "God *sent* his Son into the world, that the world through him might be saved."

Some want to protest, "Yes, but you have got to be good." Oh, we want to earn it. We want to be proud. We want to feel good about ourselves. We don't want God to do us any favors. But you can't be good enough to earn it. What we earn is death.

"The wages of sin is death, but God's free gift is eternal life in Christ Jesus our Lord."

"But," somebody will want to protest, "still you have to have a certain quality of faith. You have to go through a certain ritual. You have to do something special in order to get that forgiveness." Yes, you have to have faith—but not very much. Jesus said, ". . . faith as a grain of mustard seed," and that's the tiniest of seeds. If you wear bifocals like I do, you would probably have to take your glasses off to see a mustard seed. In order to get the forgiveness that God offers, you simply have to have enough faith to say, "I believe you love me like I am. I accept your forgiveness."

The solution to sin is forgiveness, and the result is freedom—not constraint.

Freedom, first of all, *from guilt.* Probably each of you has something in your mind that you are ashamed of, something you did when you were a child or in growing up, or something you did yesterday or last week. We spend a great deal of time saying, "I really shouldn't be ashamed of that." "It wasn't my fault anyway." "They did that to me." "It was the circumstances." "The car just did it all by itself." "People are mean." "Well, I couldn't help it." Sometimes we really should be ashamed.

Paul Tournier, the Swiss psychiatrist and a great Christian, wrote in his little book, *Guilt and Grace,* that he could get himself burdened down with the stack of medical journals that stay on his bedside table, because he never could get them all read. Have you got your stack of medical journals or professional journals or copies of *Good Housekeeping* or whatever it is you think you ought to read, and just never can keep up with? What we need to do is remember that God forgives us even for not reading professional journals. He certainly forgives us for the really evil things we do. We need to forgive ourselves, and start over again. Freedom from guilt.

And then, *freedom from the fear of exposure.* How much of our time do we spend hiding and hoping that they never find out who I really am, because if they find out what I am really like they won't like me any more? Isn't this the essential, wonderful thing about marriage: she knows me as I am, and still she loves me? Isn't that what friendship is really all about—to be known just as you are and still be loved? But we are so afraid to admit to our friends, even to our husbands and wives, that we are human beings. Sometimes we are afraid. Sometimes we are angry. Sometimes we say things we ought not to say and do things we ought not to do. Sometimes we are really distressed. Sometimes we know the agonies of depression. If we could just say, "God, forgive me for my despair. God, forgive me for my anger. God, forgive me for my evil thoughts," and then share that humanity, knowing that if

God knows and forgives, then we need not fear being known by others.

And then, *freedom from cynicism.* How many times have you had the joy just pulled out from under your feet by somebody saying just as you introduce the idea, "Oh, that won't work." "We've done that before." "They won't like it." "Nobody will come." "You'd better nail everything down and lock all the doors." "I just don't know what this generation is coming to." "Things just aren't like they used to be." People know about sin, all right. What they don't know about is forgiveness, for forgiveness makes all things new. If you and I know we are sinners and God forgives us, then what in heaven's name do you expect other people to be? If you know that you are a forgiven sinner, you don't like sin, but you can take it in stride. You expect it to be there and you expect it at least from time to time to be overcome.

And then, *freedom to love.* You know, if you are trying to hide guilt you don't have time to love anybody. You are too busy trying to figure out bad things to say about other people so you won't look so bad. You are so afraid you are going to get exposed that you have to keep all the facades up there so they won't really see you. You don't have time to love. If you are a cynic, you don't believe in love. You don't dare love anybody if you don't think they will love you back. "I am not going to love that person. Nobody is loving in this world. I am not going to dare expose myself and take that risk." But if you know you are forgiven, you have felt love, and you have felt it through the church, you have seen it demonstrated in the communion of the saints.

Did you notice that in the Apostles' Creed the communion of the saints comes first, and then the forgiveness of sins? There is a reason for that, I think. Nobody in this world has ever privately, by themselves, in solitary confinement, comprehended and accepted the love of God in Jesus Christ. We first accept the love and forgiveness of the communion of the saints, of the church around us. We can feel and maybe believe that other human beings love us, and then perhaps reach beyond that and through that to believe that God loves us. The communion of the saints comes first. Once we have accepted forgiveness, we become a part of that communion and then reach out to involve others in its warmth and life.

And then, of course, there is the *freedom from the fear of death*. We don't have to be teenagers the rest of our lives. We don't have to look young or act young or play young. If we are young, we don't have to be afraid we will die too soon, because if God forgives, we shall live forever.

The problem is sin. The solution is forgiveness. The result is freedom.

If you have never accepted the forgiveness of God, why don't you do it right now? There isn't any other solution. There isn't any other way. There isn't any other freedom. If you still have dark corners in your life, if you still have dim places you have had a hard time leaving, if you still have acts you try to hide and thoughts you could never admit, then as we sing "Just as I am, without one plea . . . ," then let the light of forgiveness shine into every single corner of your life.

The Resurrection of the Body

I Corinthians 15

Romans 6:4–11

It is sown a physical body, it is raised a spiritual body. If there is a physical body, there is also a spiritual body.

I Corinthians 15:44

The Resurrection of the Body

Life is motion. We are constantly going somewhere, reaching for something, planning something. The cells in our bodies are continuously being replaced. The blood is constantly circulating. The only real stillness is death. Even a small child sleeping moves slightly, breathing in and out. Life is motion. Consequently, the quality of life in large part is determined by the direction in which we are moving or the goals toward which we are aimed. We live our lives largely on the basis of what we expect to happen.

Last Sunday morning in "Family Circle" in the funny papers there were two panels. They were almost identical. Both showed little Billy in bed, the open window in the background, and the sun coming up. They were at precisely the same time in the morning. In the first panel the rising sun was labeled "school day." There was a little balloon above Billy's head that showed his thoughts about what he would have to do: sit in class, work a math problem, and do something he evidently didn't like. Billy was curled up in a tight knot. Even though his mother was calling him, he was determined to stay in bed as long as he could. In the second panel: same sun, same open window, same Billy. But this time the sun is labeled "vacation day," and the balloon above little Billy's head shows him running and playing with his dog outdoors in glorious freedom. Billy can't get out of that bed fast enough.

The quality of life depends upon the direction it is going, in what we expect. We who are Christians have more reason than anyone else to live the whole of life—not in a sense of gloom and downheartedness and discouragement, but in a sense of joyous expectation and anticipation of what the future will bring. In the Creed we say, "I believe in . . . the resurrection of the body; and the life everlasting." That means that we are claiming a destiny, a destiny that is good as God is good, and a destiny that applies not just to the life hereafter, but a destiny for each of us that begins in the life here and now.

Let me try then this morning to lay out what it should mean to us to say, "I believe in . . . the resurrection of the body; and the life everlasting." Sometimes an idea is easier to grasp if we can see it in contrast; so, when we talk about the resurrection of the body, let's oppose that with the *automatic immortality of the soul*. When we talk about the resurrection of the body, let's put that in contrast with the *obliteration of life and personality.* When we talk about the resurrection of the body, let's contrast that with the *reincarnation of souls.*

First of all, contrast it with the automatic immortality of the soul. If somebody were to ask you on the street, "Do you believe in the immortality of the soul?" you might answer, "Sure, every Christian believes in the immortality of the soul, but—not automatically." By the way, this is an ancient phrase, a phrase out of Greek philosophy, and it may be older than that. It is not a Christian phrase, particularly: the immortality of the soul. What that phrase means is that you will go on living pretty much like you are, regardless of what you do or how you live. The phrase is used in the fifteenth chapter of I Corinthians, but it is used after Paul talks about the resurrection of the body. It is in a chapter that is on the resurrection. He puts it this way:

> When the perishable puts on the imperishable, [there
>   has to be resurrection]
> and the mortal puts on immortality, then shall come to
>   pass the saying that is written:
> "Death is swallowed up in victory."
> "O death, where is thy victory?
> O death, where is thy sting?"

Only then is there immortality, after resurrection is given. Paul says in Romans, "For if we have been united with him in a death like his, we shall certainly be united with him in a resurrection like his." That is what is promised; not the immortality of the soul, but the resurrection of the body.

A few weeks ago I saw the very fine television production of Thornton Wilder's *Our Town*. I enjoyed it. But as a Christian, I found the last act unnecessarily sad. Do you remember the last act in *Our Town*? It takes place in the cemetery on top of the hill. All the people—the good and the bad, the prominent and the not so prominent, those who died a long time ago and those who died recently—people of all natures are there. They sit in their straight chairs like rows of gravestones at rest and at peace, in the process of forgetting all the pains of life on earth. That's what the immortality of the soul is about: not really much going on. It is not much to look forward to. It is not much to hope for. It is not much to expect. Furthermore, it is a kind of destiny in which there are no consequences. It means that there is no real earnestness about this life now. If all you are going to do is sit and rest on the top of a hill for eternity, what difference does it make, pray tell, how you live or what you do or what you don't do with this life? It is all going to be the same when we get up there on top of the hill.

When I started off to college I was scared. I had heard that college was hard. I was pretty sure that my little county high school was not as good as some of the big city high schools my classmates had graduated from. I was worried about it. I felt that I would have to study. It was better for me to be scared. I did better because I was scared. When you start a new job, it is a pretty good idea to hold real authority in some kind of awe wherever you work. If you drive an automobile, it's a good thing to be a little afraid of all that horsepower under the hood, and of all that horsepower under the hoods of those cars coming at you. It's a good thing, young and old, to be afraid of the power in alcohol when it is taken inside the human body. It can do things to you. It's a good thing to be a little in awe and a little afraid of the sex drive, because it can do good things and bad things to people. And it is good to be a little in awe—though not overawed—of life after death. I think one lives better for looking into the future with a healthy respect for consequences.

Furthermore, immortality of the soul seems to say in most people's minds, "Well, I will just be like I am forever." Think about that for a moment. On first thought, it sounds great! But, if you are going to be immortal as you are, would you be satisfied—just like you are, right now? If I were going to be immortal, I would like to take off my glasses and be able to see something more than blurred people out there. I would like to have the stamina I had when I was twenty-five. That would be kind of nice. I would like to be able to eat like I could when I was eighteen. If you are going to be immortal like you are, what about that temper that you are troubled so with? Wouldn't you just as soon rid yourself of the temper, and then be immortal? If you are painfully shy and always find yourself a little uncomfortable in new social situations, think of the myriad of people in eternity. Wouldn't you like to be a little less shy, a little more comfortable with folks? Maybe you have some other kind of personality problem that continues to plague you. Do you want to live for eternity with that? Someone has said that hell would be "having to live forever as I am."

We don't believe in the immortality of the soul. We believe in the resurrection of the body, and resurrection means transformation. It means not having to live forever as you are. It means being renewed, made whole, made like God intended you to be. That's the faithful promise worked out in Jesus Christ: not to be forever as you are, but to be forever as you can be. That's a promise worth grasping hold of, isn't it? Not the immortality of the soul, but the resurrection of the body.

But even if we talk about some fear and awe, let us remember that we are not talking as Christians about obliteration any more than we are talking about automatic immortality. We are Christians who live in confidence about what the future holds, for the promises are real. Paul says, "For if we have been united with him in a death like his, we shall certainly be united with him in a resurrection like his."

All you need to do to be eligible for the resurrection is to say, "Lord, I trust you, that your death is for me. I believe." But do you know what that implies? Paul said that it means to be crucified with Christ. Why did Christ die? He died because of sin, didn't he? He died because people could not make it on their own. He died because sin had so caught up and enslaved people, as Paul talks about it here in Romans, that we human beings could not work it out for ourselves and make it by ourselves. To say, "I believe, I accept your death for me," means to say, "Lord, I can't do it. I have tried all my life to make it come right by doing it myself, and it won't work. I get the brightest visions, but I can't reach up to them. I can set the best of goals, and I not only cannot accomplish them, I can't even remember them. I say I am going to drop this bad habit, and in five minutes I have forgotten that I made the vow to drop it. Lord, there just isn't any health in me, and I give up on myself, and I accept your death for me. Lord, I can't change myself. You will have to change me."

That's faith. That's being crucified with Christ. That's letting the old self die because you have given up on it. That's where you can start again. The promise is, not just that there will be life for eternity, but it will be your life fulfilled for eternity. That which is really you will be resurrected and transformed and will survive—not some unconscious, numbered spirit up there in some cubbyhole to take your place, not some color-coded ghost that is up there for you, but really *you*. Remember the promise that Jesus gave to the thief on the cross: "Today *you* will be with me in paradise." That's what the resurrection of the body means—not this same physical body we have now, but the spiritual body that Paul promises; a transformed body, but, nevertheless, a recognizable body. You will know who you are, you will know who other people are, and they will recognize you.

Remember God speaking to Moses, saying, "I am the God of Abraham and of Isaac and of Jacob." He did not say, "I was the God of these people who were." He said, "I *am* the God" of these men (Abraham, Isaac, and Jacob) who died and yet *are,* and are identifiable. When Jesus himself was raised from the dead—raised bodily—and Thomas came to him in doubt, Jesus said, "Thomas, put your finger in the nail print." It was still there. "Thrust your hand in my side, and be not faithless, but believing." Because Jesus was resurrected in the body, so will you be.

Paul gets into a veritable litany in talking about that which is changed:

What is sown is perishable [that is, this body on earth],
   what is raised is imperishable.
It is sown in dishonor, it is raised in glory.
It is sown in weakness, it is raised in power.
It is sown a physical body, it is raised a spiritual body.

Believe me, I don't know what all that means, but I
know that it means that *you*—specifically, uniquely—*you*
will survive, be resurrected, transformed, and made whole
forever.

If you and I shall be identifiable, transformed beings in
the life to come, then that sets a different course for us in
the life we now have. If you are going to be obliterated,
then you might as well "eat, drink, and be merry, for tomorrow you die." Let me tell you something. Those who
live that way have not found the secret to the new life.
They have not discovered how to be joyous and happy.
The truth is: those who eat and drink to be merry have not
found anything else that can give them joy except perhaps
the next round of drinks and the next cruise on the Carib-
bean and the next flight to Europe and the next activity.
Those who know that they shall be resurrected and transformed and made whole can transform a simple breakfast
around the family table. They can transform the most ordinary kind of work. They can find happiness sitting on
the front porch or on the back steps talking with a neighbor.

Late one winter, when I was in seminary, we got tired
of studying, tired of classes, tired of writing papers, tired
of taking tests, and tired of keeping a schedule. Somebody
said, "Let's go to the mountains for the spring holiday."

Somebody said, "I have a brochure on state parks." Somebody else mentioned Vogel. At about that point, my roommate said, "Wait a minute." He went over to the closet, still talking, as he was rummaging around in there. "I have a hat I always wear when we talk about things like this." He came out with an old battered white fishing hat, clamped it down on his head, to the immense satisfaction of all present, and said, "Now I am ready to talk about going to the mountains in the spring." If you know where you are going for eternity, you might just as well start wearing your "resurrection hat" right now.

There is one other contrast that needs to be made. To say that we believe in the resurrection of the body means that we do not believe in the reincarnation of souls. A few years ago it would not have occurred to anyone to bring that subject up in a Christian pulpit in America when talking about the Apostles' Creed, but that old Hindu idea of the reincarnation of souls keeps cropping up and fascinating people. It is very different from the Christian gospel. The reincarnation of souls means simply this: you live this life and you are rewarded or punished by living a better life or a lesser life the next time around. That is to say, if you live a good life, the next time you get to be a saint or a ruler or someone of more culture or more intelligence or of a higher class. If you don't live that life so well, the third time around you may slip back into somebody of a lower class, or less intelligence. If you are bad, you might return as an animal. That's the reason they are so careful about the water buffalos and the cows in India. They just might be their ancestors. If you are really bad you might end up being an insect; but if you are a good fly, then the fourth or fifth time around you might get back up into humanity. So it goes, on and on, over and over again, throughout eternity, except for a very few special individuals who finally bubble over at the top and slip over into a period of rest.

The gospel is in drastic contrast to this. Jesus Christ died for us, once and for all. By his righteousness we are recognized as righteous, once and for all. The sins which we have committed are forgiven in him, once and for all. There is no distinction in reward or punishment. There is no half reward, no elevator to go up, living one life after another in order to get to heaven. "*Today* you shall be with me in paradise." There are no stages in between in Christ Jesus.

Further, there are no second chances either. This is our only life here on earth. As far as we know, there is no chance to live as another person, no second chance to believe. This life is real and earnest, and Jesus Christ is all we need. The promises he made are for eternity, starting immediately after death. All die, but those who are in Christ Jesus shall be raised to eternal life—the first time. No ifs, ands, or buts; no equivocation. There is no coming back.

I have never been to India, but I perceive from listening and reading that there is a kind of spiritual fatigue and listlessness throughout that whole continent. Wouldn't listlessness be natural if all that can be promised after living this life is that you get up just a little bit higher in another life and then in another life and in another life? The whole thing makes me weary. Besides, you always know that you could slip back. That, it seems to me, would imply the exercise of caution—not daring—in the spiritual life. Furthermore, if someone above you is living the life that it was given to them to live in reincarnation, there is no use in your trying to be like them, because the only way you can get there is in another life. And if somebody is pretty bad and lives in a low estate and needs help, there is not much point in helping him, because he is destined to lead that life until he can be good and get into a better life in another estate. You can see why India continues to have the caste system and the poverty it has, as well as a seeming lack of caring. Whenever the belief in the reincarnation of souls exists, there must be a kind of listlessness and hopelessness.

Some have said that in western Europe and in the United States of America we operate with optimism and a sense of anticipation for the future—ready to move out, to achieve, to serve God and to give him glory—because of the good climate of the northern temperate zone. Well, the climate has probably helped, but what has really made the difference is that there have been a great many men and women in Christian Europe and in Christian America who knew exactly where they were going and knew what kind of destiny they had, both hereafter and in this life. They have been taught and made to believe since childhood that they could live with joy and anticipation, walk not only through this valley of the shadow of death for eternity, but walk through all the valleys of shadows of this life, certain and sure about the God who walks with them and ahead of them. They have made a difference in the ways that whole nations have lived.

I believe in . . . the resurrection of the body; and in the life everlasting.

When we come together in church and baptize a baby, we not only look backward, we look forward. We believe that God in his Spirit has already begun to work in the life of that child. We are also confident that God in his Spirit will continue to work in the life of that child through this life and through eternity. We believe that we as parents, by the grace of God, will be a part of the movement of his Spirit.

When we come to the Lord's Table and we sit and break the bread and drink the wine, we are, of course, looking back and remembering Jesus' broken body and shed blood, his sacrifice for our sins; but we are also looking forward in anticipation to the glorious banquet of the Lamb in the totally fulfilled Kingdom of God in the future. It is an anticipatory meal in which we sense and talk about the promises of the life to come, both in this world and the next. When we join together in worship singing our hymns, reading our Scripture, and hearing our sermons, we are reminded again of Jesus Christ crucified for our sins and of the grace of God that makes us whole. We are also aware that we look forward in joyous anticipation to that day when we shall sing our doxology, our hymn of praise, our "Jerusalem the Golden," and all the rest, with all that grand host of apostles and prophets and saints, and the just ordinary down-to-earth Christians who have gone before us and who walk alongside us. We will spend eternity feasting and becoming reacquainted with all whom we have known in this life, and having that great and glorious privilege of becoming acquainted with the myriad of Christians who have gone before us that we have not seen and with whom we have not yet enjoyed fellowship. Throughout all eternity that shall be done in the pleasant company of our Lord—for ever and ever.

If you have given up on yourself and let the will to do it your way die, crucified with Christ, then you are being changed. You will be totally changed and you will live forever. No one can take that away from you, for Jesus Christ is risen from the dead and so will you. We believe in the resurrection of the body and the life everlasting.

Amen and amen.

Index of Scriptural References

Subject Index

Second Coming of Christ, 151–58
Simon Peter. *See* Peter
Sins, forgiveness of, 207–15
Speed, Flora, 8
Spence, Hartzel, 59
"Suffered under Pontius Pilate," 101–8

Temple, Archbishop William, 154
Thomas (apostle), 135, 225
Thomas, Pat, 8

Tongues, speaking in, 31, 171, 193
Tournier, Paul, 213

Unity, 195–96

Westminster Confession of Faith, 165, 166
Wilder, Thornton, 222

Yellowstone National Park, 52

About the Author

Dr. James O. Speed has been pastor of First Presbyterian Church in Marietta, Georgia, for the past fifteen years and has been in the ministry for thirty years.

Dr. Speed was born December 7, 1930, in Mobile, Alabama, the son of J. O. and Mary Speed. When he was very young, his parents moved to Birmingham, Alabama, where his father was an elder in the South Highland Presbyterian Church. Dr. Speed was graduated cum laude from Davidson College in 1953 and from Columbia Theological Seminary, again with honors, in 1957. He received his Doctorate of Ministry from Columbia Seminary in June of 1984.

Ordained by the Presbytery of East Alabama in 1957, Dr. Speed served as assistant pastor of Trinity Presbyterian

Church in Montgomery and then as pastor of the First Presbyterian Church of Alexander City, Alabama.

From 1960 to 1964, Dr. Speed served on the staff of the Board of Christian Education in Richmond, Virginia, and from 1964 until 1972 as minister of Trinity Presbyterian Church in Birmingham, Alabama. In July 1972, he accepted the call of the First Presbyterian Church in Marietta.

Since coming to Marietta, Dr. Speed has been chairman of the Council of the Synod of the Southeast, moderator of the Cherokee Presbytery, chairman of the Council on Theology and Culture of the Presbyterian Church, U.S., and a member of the board of trustees of Presbyterian College.

Dr. Speed has also served as president of the Marietta Rotary Club and three times as chaplain of the Rotary District. He is a past president of the board of the Cobb County Symposium, a member of the board of the Marietta-Cobb Girls Club, and on the board of Cobb Emergency Aid. Dr. Speed is a trustee of A Christian Ministry in the National Parks, one of his major interests since serving as an intern at Crater Lake and Death Valley in his seminary days.

Dr. Speed enjoys jogging several times a week and backpacking when his schedule permits. He has participated in three Explorer Scout and Presbytery High Adventure expeditions to the Philmont Scout Ranch in New Mexico, and in the summer of 1986, he was a chaplain on the Philmont staff.

Dr. Speed is married to the former Flora McDonald of Tallapoosa, Georgia, and they have four grown children: Beth, Mary, Sarah, and Todd.